What Ever Know Abou

When a man becomes a father, it can be a very daunting time. He is suddenly thrust into a new and emotional world. He can feel unprepared (despite the preceding nine months of build-up), useless (despite all the 'uses' the mother of his child could offer him), and apprehensive. However, the new father is about to embark upon the most exciting and rewarding experience of his life. But let's face it, no one teaches men exactly how to become fathers.

So, what does being a dad in the twenty-first century mean? Dads today, more than ever, want to play an active role in their children's lives and development. To do this, fathers need to know how children grow up so that they can learn to cope with, play, control, and love their kids in an intelligent way.

This book provides a guide for men on how to be a good dad and a supportive partner. Dealing directly with the key issues and the many stresses that fathers can face, it looks at the psychological research on child development, parenting, and fathering in particular. It examines such thorny topics as stepfatherhood, the changing relationship between partners, and sex after babies. It also offers valuable advice on problems all dads will face – how to bond, how to provide sensible discipline, learning to play, and managing teenage tantrums and traumas.

The author, David Cohen, is a psychologist. In a quirky and anecdotal style, and drawing on wide research, this book tells men everything they need to know about being a dad.

David Cohen trained as a psychologist and has worked as a writer and film maker. He set up Psychology News as a magazine which has since become a film and TV production company as well as a publisher. He is, as you remain all your life, a father and stepfather.

PARENT AND CHILD SERIES
Edited by David Cohen

This series aims to bridge the gap in parents' understanding of the issues that may affect their children from infancy to early adolescence. These scientifically grounded books will communicate the findings of psychologists and other developmental experts to parents in a user-friendly way.

The books will be brief but comprehensive, accessible and intelligent. Topics will cover both normal development and problem areas, such as nutrition, sexuality, eating disorders, learning disabilities, aggressive children and conduct disorders, drugs and alcohol use, and relationship building. The books will be invaluable for all parents and parents-to-be.

FORTHCOMING BOOKS IN THE SERIES

Strahan, Dixon and Banks/*Parenting with Reason: Evidence-Based Approaches to Parenting Dilemmas* (October 2009)
A rich common-sense manual on "evidence-based parenting." Grounded in the best research available, it provides parents with the evidence to help them make the "tough parenting decisions" that they face.

Sonna/*First Friends: Nurturing your Child's Social Development* (Summer 2010)
Toddlers' social issues are as many and varied as children themselves. This book gives parents the tools to teach their children what they need to know: how to get along with others and form healthy, satisfying relationships.

What Every Man Should Know About Being a Dad

David Cohen

Routledge
Taylor & Francis Group

LONDON AND NEW YORK

First published 2009
by Routledge
27 Church Road, Hove, East Sussex BN3 2FA

Simultaneously published in the USA and Canada
by Routledge
270 Madison Avenue, New York, NY 10016

Routledge is an imprint of the Taylor & Francis Group, an Informa business

Typeset in New Century Schoolbook by Garfield Morgan,
Swansea, West Glamorgan
Printed and bound in Great Britain by TJ International Ltd
Padstow, Cornwall
Cover design by Mark Woods

British Library Cataloguing in Publication Data
A catalogue record for this book is available from the British Library

Library of Congress Cataloging in Publication Data
Cohen, David, 1946–
  What every man should know about being a dad / David Cohen.
    p. cm. – (Parent and child)
  Includes bibliographical references and index.
  ISBN 978-0-415-48616-3 (hb) – ISBN 978-0-415-48617-0 (soft cover)
1. Fatherhood. 2. Father and child. I. Title.
  HQ756.C622 2009
  649'.10851–dc22

                                                          2009003825

ISBN 978-0-415-48616-3 (hbk)
ISBN 978-0-415-48617-0 (pbk)

Contents

Joy

Source: www.CartoonStock.com

After you become a father, you'll be:
Crying
Crying with laughter
Crying with joy
Crying with fear.

There is a Yiddish proverb:

So you have no children?
What then do you do for aggravation?

Philip Larkin would have smiled at that. His great poem *Dockery and Son* muses on the fact he had no children himself.

> To have no son, no wife,
> No house or land still seemed quite natural.
> Only a numbness registered the shock
> Of finding out how much had gone of life.[1]

Larkin liked being a spectator, safe on the sidelines of life. If you like the sidelines, you shouldn't become a dad. As a father you will live with all the pleasures and pains, ups and downs, highs and lows, of life. You'll never be 100 per cent safe because you'll never be able to protect your children from every danger.

My sons are in their thirties now and I still worry about them. Are they happy? Is their work going okay? Do they have money in the bank?

We live in confused, confusing times. On the one hand, 27 million children in America have to cope with 'father absence' which is linked to poverty, failure in school, teen pregnancy, substance abuse, violent crime and depression. On the other hand, millions of fathers all over the world want to be more involved.

You're not likely to be reading this book if you have no interest in being a good dad. In Britain, you are also no longer likely to be that young. The average age for a first-time father is 32 years. In most Western European countries the trend is the same. Many men want to concentrate on their careers.

One bizarre, and one very positive, development. Let's do the bizarre first. Ninety per cent of a rather small sample of 31 expectant dads in Newfoundland suffered nausea, weird food cravings and put on weight. These men had much higher levels of prolactin than normal, prolactin being the hormone which produces milk in new mothers. Prolactin also prompts birds to build nests.

---

1 'Dockery and Son' from *The Whitsun Weddings* by Philip Larkin. © Faber and Faber Ltd, reproduced with permission.

The positive is that more men attend the birth of their children than ever before. In 1970, one man in five in the UK was present. By 1980 that had doubled. Today, 93 per cent of fathers who live with their partners do so, but what is perhaps even more telling is that 45 per cent of fathers who are not living with the mother still attend the birth (Kiernan and Smith, 2003). Nearly half (48 per cent) of fathers-to-be go to antenatal or parenting classes and 85 per cent go to at least one prenatal appointment with a midwife, or one ultrasound scan (National Health Service, 2005). The same is true in America, France, Germany, Holland, Japan and many other countries. All over the world dads have never been less on the sidelines with Larkin.

Being in at the birth is, for many men, a peak experience, something they will remember till the day they die. I can still summon my intense, magical memories of the births of Nicholas and Reuben. Fathers who are present at the birth will bond more easily with their babies.

Remember that when you're standing at the Cash Denuding Machine, hoping it will give you £50 for nappies and toys. Remember that, when you read the grim stats. The average British parent spends something like £80,000 on the average child by the time said child gets to 18. Some estimates put it up to £150,000. But, British, American and others fathers, spare a moment for the chick-pecked Italian papa. What follows could make an opera called *Umberto's Hair*.

In 2008, at the age of 22, Umberto decided he'd had enough of working in an abattoir and de-boning pigs. He wanted to do perms rather than pigs. Like many Italians, Umberto was still living at home with mama. Papa had left and now withdrew the all-important wallet; he had no intention of subbing Umberto to become a hairdresser.

Umberto was not going to just sulk. He hired a lawyer who told him to sue Dad as it is the inalienable right of every Italian boy to have papa fork out. The Court supported Umberto. So Dad has to cough up 300 euros a month until his son has the coiff-ology or the permit to perm. I picture a touching death bed scene. Dad says he is sorry; father and son embrace; Umberto gives his father one last hair cut before the old man pops his clogs. All set to music!

Umberto's dad is not the only dad put in the dock by a son. In my twenties, I worked for the Paris-based film producer Alexander Salkind who made *Superman*. When he was dying, his son was suing him for $6 million dollars which makes the Umberto case seem small paternal potatoes.

Enough of the negatives! Fatherhood has so many joys beyond seeing your kids born. To the day I die, I won't forget the high when my six-month-old son and I laughed at each other for hours. I won't forget my pride when my other son, aged three, was given puzzles by the head teacher of a posh kindergarten. He looked seriously at her and said 'Ah, it's my exam.' She laughed; I laughed. 'I think he's just passed with flying colours,' she smiled. Many of my best experiences have come out of being a father.

Yet I had many reasons to fear I would be a lousy dad. This book is not one of that new genre – the misery memoir or 'Painful Lives' – but some of my personal history left me with 'issues'.

Home alone

When I was ten, I used to hate coming back from school and not finding my mother at home. I never knew where she was. She did not work. We had just moved to London from Geneva and I was finding my prep school weird. I had never been to an English school before and some of the behaviour of boys and masters left me flabbergasted. One teacher kept flicking matches at us; another one beat us if we got our Latin verbs wrong and, also, if we got our Latin verbs right, so that we wouldn't get too uppity.

I developed a magical obsessional ritual for dealing with my anxieties. If my mother wasn't home, I'd walk round our block of flats and a nearby square twice. It was all down to will power. If I didn't take a peep through the living-room window – we lived on the ground floor – to see if she was back, then she would be back home after my second walk around. The walk took about eight minutes.

More often than not, my ritual failed. She hadn't appeared. I'd then walk to Marble Arch and back. If that failed, I went as far as Baker Street – and then walked back.

I had not really conquered this anxiety two years later. Then suddenly everything changed. Just after my thirteenth birthday, my father begged me to persuade my mother to go to Israel to sell a flat they still owned there. He had been a lawyer but had gone into business and the business was not going well. He'd go bankrupt if she didn't do it. Their marriage was unhappy; my mother distrusted him. She suspected he wanted her out of the country so he could canoodle with secretaries. (She called them sex-retaries.) My father told me I was now grown up enough to understand that he needed my help to make my mother see sense. Her family had warped her.

Eventually, my mother gave in to his pressure, my pressure and flew to Israel. After the first few days, my father often had to be away overnight. A businessman could not ignore 'business opportunities', he explained and there were many in Manchester, Birmingham and other far-off cities. I wasn't a baby. He'd be back tomorrow. And, at first, he always was.

After a few weeks, however, the electricity in the flat failed. My father couldn't fix a fuse though he could discourse on Benjamin Franklin and lightning in the Old Testament. Jehovah is electric, kneel! The fuse crisis became his justification for moving out. After that, I lived on my own in a luxury flat in the West End. The porter got an electrician in case you're worrying I lived in the dark. My father never asked me not to tell my mother he had gone. I missed her terribly and wrote desperate letters.

Once I told her, in a frantic telegram followed by a frantic letter, he had gone, I expected her to fly back at once. I couldn't understand why she didn't tell me when she was coming back. But days passed, weeks passed and she still hadn't closed the sale.

My father didn't abandon me totally. Sometimes, he came back to spend a night in the flat. I was always welcome at his office in Jermyn Street. Every Friday we ate together at smart restaurants like the *Ecu de France*, near Piccadilly. My father liked it because General De Gaulle liked to eat there during the war. Benjamin Cohen OBE would ask me what had happened at school and give me £10 housekeeping for the week. In the early 1960s, this was a fabulous sum. By 10 o'clock, I was back at the flat, alone.

I was lonely and confused. As the weeks passed, I was terrified my school would find out what had happened. I knew 13-year-olds were not meant to live alone. I couldn't tell anyone.

I am amazed I had the sense to get my school uniform well pressed by Jeff Bell of Seymour Dry Cleaners who kept on asking how my mother was, but then, tactfully, stopped asking. For years afterwards I hated dry cleaners. I had to learn how to cook or I'd be condemned to a life of TV dinners. My father arranged for a cleaning lady and, later, for an au pair to live in the flat. I lusted after Monica, the Finnish au pair, but she had a boyfriend and, after three months, went off to live with him.

From the age of 13 to the age of 16, I lived by myself in my grand flat just off Marble Arch. I often cried myself to sleep. I kept writing to my mother and I made what I now recognise were cries for help. Once, I turned up at synagogue in rugby shorts; the rabbi didn't ask why I did such a peculiar thing. He just told me to tell my mother never again to let me come to God's temple improperly dressed. At night, I sometimes roamed the West End streets. Inevitably, I was picked up by men but I was so innocent that I had no idea what they were after at first.

One of my more comic crises was hair-linked. After I washed my hair, the bath-tub was full of hair. Not only had I driven my parents away but my head would soon be as bald as a baby's bum. No girl would ever look at me. Then, I saw an ad in the *Evening Standard* that promised a cure.

The trichologist, or magical hair restorer, had a stern receptionist, just like the dentist; he wore a white suit, just like the dentist. As soon as he saw me, he sighed. Oh dear, he had rarely seen such a dangerous case. If I didn't go in for the full treatment, I'd be bald in a matter of months. I said I only had £20 on me – then about two weeks of the average national wage.

But since I was so young, the kindly hair magician agreed to start the treatment just for that. Normally he took £50, he said, but I was a tragic case. The hair guru ran an electric comb which made my scalp tingle, lathered me with weird stuff and sold me hugely expensive red goo. Never in my life have I shampooed so faithfully.

It worked. I still have a full head of hair. Can anyone prove to me it wasn't the treatment that did it? Teenage neurotics sometimes get it right!

At school I swotted. It was partly pride, partly fear, partly not much else do. Erik Erikson, a psychiatrist whose stages of development I will cover later, argues that as teenagers we choose between industry and inferiority. I chose industry. My parents might have walked out on me but I could write essays on Luther, Calvin, transubstantiation, King Lear, Elizabeth I, Molière and why Charles I was so stubborn that he lost his head.

My worst school ordeal was military, not academic. Every Monday we had to parade in the cadet corps. Field Marshal Montgomery had been to my old school and the corps was compulsory. I couldn't march properly, I couldn't present arms and when I tried to shoot it was a disaster. But I was becoming wily; I started to forge absentee notes many Mondays. No one at school ever asked why I was always sick on Mondays. I reckoned I had every right to play truant.

Children who live alone are at risk from many dangers. I was not a victim of strange men but I was a victim of a cooking pot. I decided I must learn to cook. And there was a pressure cooker in the kitchen. I did something wrong, the lid blew off and I got burned. I took a taxi to St George's Hospital, one of London's famous teaching hospitals. No one asked why a 13-year-old boy should turn up in casualty alone late in the evening. In those days, no one had heard of battered baby syndrome, child sexual abuse, stepfathers who raped their stepkids, or emotional abuse.

I was patched up and got another taxi home. I didn't even bother to ring my father. The hospital certainly didn't. No one from social services came either.

I saw my mother a number of times during these three years. The sale of the house was very complicated and the contract had never been finalised. So she could not come home yet, she told me. It was a lie. She had met a millionaire.

I learned about girls. Eventually, when I was 15, I met Judith who was 20. Her mother had died and, within two weeks, she had moved into my flat. I wasn't lonely any more. I now had to hide from my school the altogether amazing fact that I was living with a woman.

Don't imagine my parents felt guilty. They may have been the only Jews in history who didn't experience crippling guilt. Making crippling demands was a different matter; at that they were experts. When they divorced, they asked me to negotiate the financial details between them. My father complained my mother had deluded ideas about how rich he was; my mother complained he had lied to her for years. I tried to hammer out a fair deal between them. They were impossible. I ended up threatening to throw myself off the balcony of my mother's flat if she did not finally sign the deal. I was 20 years old and at the end of my tether. The balcony wasn't that high, about 12 feet off the ground, so I was more likely to break an ankle than to die, but my distress was real enough.

I've written at length about this because being left was a turning point for me. It damaged my relationship with both my parents, especially with my mother to whom I had been very close. I found it hard to forgive her and it did not help that she would never discuss it because she was so bitter herself about her own failed marriage. The millionaire also failed her; he died just after she had agreed to marry him and before he changed his will in her favour.

But my parents had their parents. My father's father had spent most of his adult life away from his home. My mother adored her father who was something of a philanderer.

As my parents grew old and, then, very old, I wanted to forgive them. But I wanted something back. I wanted them to explain why they had done it, but we never really dealt with the stark truth that they had left me when I was so young.

I would love to be able to write that in the end there was perfect love and true forgiveness. As I got into my thirties I did forgive them – sort of. I realised they had their own side to it – sort of. But it was far from total forgiveness. I wouldn't wish any teenager to go through that kind of experience even though I learned things about myself as well as some useful strategies for not cracking under pressure. I always got up to face the day.

But I also learned to put up with betrayals perhaps more than I should. I had managed the separation from my parents reasonably. I hadn't gone mad or taken hundreds of pills. But the fear of separation stayed with me. I can still see traces of that in me now.

Eventually I went to Oxford University but found I could not cope with doing the Tudors and Stuarts again, with Luther and Calvin again. I switched to psychology and philosophy and became very interested in child psychology. I got my doctorate with a thesis on children's laughter and how that affects their social and emotional development. I wrote books on Piaget, the most influential child psychologist of the twentieth century, and on psychometric testing. I also started to make TV documentaries, a number of them on child abuse.

I tried at one point to write a book about being left home alone but publishers said that, alas, I had been insufficiently abused for it to work as a misery memoir. I had just been abandoned, not raped, violated, beaten to a pulp by a drunken stepdad or subjected to bizarre spiritual occult practices. No one wanted a book called, a friend of mine suggested, *No One Hit Me Hard Enough*.

Being abandoned did make me very determined in one way. I was not going to let my own damaged childhood damage my children.

Upper class twist

I suggested a book which looked at research on fathering in the early 1980s, but, again, no one wanted to commission it. Men simply would not be seen with such a book – particularly not in Britain where men would run to the pub if they were asked to change a nappy. There was a peculiarly British twist as well. The upper middle and upper classes have been sending their children to boarding school for the last 150 years.

When Aileen and my sons went to Dulwich College Preparatory School, the Headmaster, Hugh Woodcock, told us at a parents' evening that he had had to draw the line. Enough was enough. Some parents had asked if their children could board while they were still in kindergarten. That really was not on, Woodcock said. Until a child was five he, or she, needed to be at home. Though many had nannies, one reason the upper and upper middle classes sent their children away was to protect their freedom. If they had to pick Harry up from school that might interfere with their shopping, polo or extramarital affairs.

These parents were right about the loss of freedom. Becoming a father means you can't do everything else you might want to. Our narcissistic culture makes many 20- and 30-year-olds wonder if having children is worth the hassle. Will being a parent mean less time for playing five a side or pub visiting? Might I have to spend so many hours changing nappies and sterilising bottles, I'll be too pooped (excuse the pun) to develop my latest ideas in video-gaming? I might have to give up so much.

I've heard these siren voices. Maybe, if I hadn't become a father at 24, I would have made more memorable films, or written the novel I like to believe I always had in me . . . but I don't mind one bit. So reader be warned. This book is objective about the research on fathering, objective about social trends but I'm not objective about being a dad. For me that has been one of the best, if not the actually best, experience of my life. I thank Aileen La Tourette, mother of my children, for helping make it happen.

This book covers attitudes to becoming a father and the latest research on things every dad should know – how children's minds develop, what parents must do to bond with their children, how children learn to pretend and to lie, on the personality of children, on sexual development, on how to help children at school and how to cope when they become teenagers. It also traces how social attitudes have changed and most half-honest men will admit that is mainly the result of feminism. While some feminists were hostile to men, many claimed men lost out by not being very involved with their children. I agree with that.

This is not a book of dogmatic advice because being a father requires imagination and the ability to deal with unexpected situations. But I have included 19 sections marked *Self Analysis*. Fathers today need to be self aware apart from everything else they need to be. And the text is also peppered with sections called Silly Games. Research on how children develop suggests many games dads can play with their children – as long as you lose your inhibitions about looking like a perfect idiot. There are times when a good dad simply has to be a perfect idiot.

2

You are not a spare part whatever psychologists say

Two of the last three Presidents of the United States – Bill Clinton and Barack Obama – hardly had any relationship with their fathers. Clinton had a problematic relationship with a stepfather who drank too much. Obama writes movingly that he was brought up by his mother and grandfather; he last saw his father when he was a toddler; his grandfather was a disappointed man because he had not done well as an insurance salesman. In terms of fathering the Presidential experience is bad news because it suggests that dad really is a spare part. Psychology is an inexact business and some individuals are just exceptional. Not all Presidents of the United States come into that last category.

Books on how to be a good parent have existed since the days of ancient Greece but all of them have focused on the role of the mother. Psychologists, as we shall see, also focused much more on mothers apart from Freud of whom more later. But Freud didn't really tell fathers how to bring up children. He merely argued that young boys often have unconscious fears their fathers will castrate them!

In *Reassessing Fatherhood* (Lewis and O'Brien, 1987), the authors argued the 1970s saw much new research on fatherhood. The rise of feminism had made it obvious to psychologists they should analyse why men did rather little. Despite the impact feminism had on many of us, the lives of young parents had not changed dramatically by the mid 1980s. The children were very much women's work, as I found out in 1980, when I made a film, *When Men Become Mothers*. I interviewed men who had been forced to become full-time fathers when their wives left them. These men were confused and angry; most had to abandon their careers. Their social lives did not exactly fizz either. Women often did not want to go out with them because they suspected these men wanted help looking after their kids more than a hot date.

There's also an academic oddity. Many writers on masculinity approach the subject from a gay perspective. Gay writers are not usually that concerned about fatherhood. So women have written more on fathers than men have. My favourite feminist-on-fathers text is by two Dutch

Source: www.CartoonStock.com

psychotherapists. *Unravelling the Father* includes a chapter titled 'Father is a money bag'. Prepare for that experience, dads. Think of yourself as a piggy bank which is constantly raided.

The Dutch authors stress many fathers admit they have 'negative qualities as a father'. The poor schmucks own up to 'a lack of relational capacities, a lack of involvement' and so do not really contribute much to bringing up their children. This is an extreme view, of course.

Research on fathering does not make glorious reading. Dads often are found to be lazy, selfish and inconsistent. For example, when Charlie Lewis looked at what men did for their one-year-olds, the results were depressing: 62 per cent of fathers never helped bathe their child, 53 per cent never looked after their child on their own, and now for what I must confess is my favourite finding, 40 per cent of dads had never changed a nappy. One should not underestimate the shock a full nappy may cause to a red-blooded man. One father admitted he could not change a nappy because 'I would vomit on the spot at the sight of the poo.' His unhappy experiences mucking out a guinea pig cage had left him traumatised.

If Kafka's dad had been a penguin

In *The Emperor's Embrace* (1999), Jeffrey Masson claimed human fathers have much to learn from wolves, lions and, especially, emperor penguins. The king of all fathers is the emperor penguin who warms the egg on his feet for months, so keeping nipper penguin safe from the icy Antarctic climate. Ma Penguin is a major feminist and swims the frozen seas looking for food. While cuddling the nipper, Pa Penguin doesn't care how nippy it gets. And he starves. This is devoted fatherhood indeed! Masson asked his readers to compare the experience of the infant penguin with that of the Jewish writer, Franz Kafka, who complained his father bullied him. And never gave him the best cuts of fish.

If his dad had been a penguin, Kafka would have been happier though he probably wouldn't have written his masterpiece, *The Trial*. Its hero, Joseph K, is never told what he is accused of, but still feels guilty. Some critics argue the book owes much to Kafka's unhappy relationship with his father who always made him feel guilty . . .

Psychology has failed to study fathers and fathering as much as it ought to have done but, at least, it has offered insights into Kafka's guilt. One of the most famous, if controversial, concepts in psychology – Freud's Oedipus Complex – argues every male child wants to kill his father and sleep with his mother. Unconsciously. So we assume that this is what Kafka dreaded he was really on trial for. No wonder it is easy for sons to feel guilty.

Feeling guilty about their swinish, unforgivable lusts, little boys imagine their dad wants to castrate them. Daughters have a complex of their own, the Electra Complex. They don't seem to insist on killing their mothers as long as they sleep with their dads.

The absent father syndrome

War has sometimes provided psychologists with extreme conditions to test hypotheses. In the late 1940s, they examined how children, whose fathers had been away fighting, did both on intelligence tests and at school. In general, if fathers had been absent their children did less well intellectually and in terms of emotional adjustment, That was especially true if the child had been very young when the father was absent.

Williams and Radin (1999) found that both the quantity and quality of time fathers spent with their four-year-old boys correlated with intelligence test scores. The strongest link was with so-called 'paternal nurturance'. Children whose dads cared, children whose dads reached out, did much better socially and intellectually. Black girls and boys in elementary school did better on every kind of test the more their parents interacted with the children. The father's behaviour was especially important for boys.

Social class was also a factor. Working-class children were more affected than middle-class children by the father's absence. Elementary-school boys who were one or two years behind at school had very poor relationships with their fathers; their fathers were inadequate, had failed to achieve their own ambitions and transmitted that failure to their sons. If dad was not there, language skills and perceptual motor and manipulative skills were also damaged (Lessing *et al.*, 1970).

The problem is international. In 2008, Scotland Yard issued a report which claimed there were 151 teenage gangs in London. Senior policemen – and many have studied psychology – argue boys don't have good male role models: dad is not there, so the gang, or the gang leader, becomes a substitute father.

Daughters who grow up with no father around also have problems. Like boys their cognitive development is harmed as is their performance at school (Grimm-Wassil, 1994, p. 149). Their maths skills suffer especially, he found.

The age at which a daughter loses her father is meaningful since it influences her perception of males and the world as well as her academic advancement. The younger a girl is when her father leaves or dies, the less strong her sense of security is. More girls who lose their dads become teenage mothers too. Griffin argues that a key factor is that such girls have less sense of stability and that the absence of a father makes it harder for them to make sensible decisions. It also makes it more likely, when they face crises, for them to have negative reactions as opposed to positive ones (Griffin, 1998, p. 26). A confident base enables girls to be successful academically, he claims.

The feminist writer Rosalind Miles argued in *The Children We Deserve* (1994) that most men, not just Kafka's dad, cannot fulfil the basic requirement of parenting. Jealous sex-mad little boys that we men are, we cannot give total, unconditional love. Children always have to prove themselves to the 'old man' if he is to love them and the old man sets up obstacles because he gets jealous. Once a child is born, the 'old man' will never be No. 1 again. Miles comes close to suggesting that no man is capable of loving his children properly.

I am not sure what total, unconditional love means but I think I know what loving children through thick and thin involves – spending time with them, talking to them, never not returning their phone calls, giving them reassurance, telling them they look great when they do and, sometimes, when they don't, endless practical as well as emotional support. James Watson, the son of the psychologist, John B. Watson (who founded a school known as behaviourism), told me he loved doing woodwork with his father. That was the best of times. James showed me the beautiful barrel-shaped barn they built together in Westport, Connecticut.

Love is woodwork – well, maybe

I am not suggesting doing woodwork is enough to show love, but it's exactly the kind of activity that makes up *good enough fathering*.

Forget Freud, his Oedipus Complex, his Schmoedipus Complex or his Octopus Complex (which I have just invented because writers on psychology must have the freedom to fangle up new complexes). Some shrinks talk of the family 'nexus', the tentacles of family life, which can strangle our souls and our selves. Some of the most useful psychoanalytic ideas on parenting come from D.W. Winnicott (1896–1971). He argued babies thrived as long as they got good enough mothering. The good enough mother is not perfect but she is attuned to her baby; she adapts as the baby develops. Good enough mothering, Winnicott claimed, gives the baby and then the toddler some sense of control, of his own power and of identity while still enjoying the comfort of being connected with his mother. But as the baby develops, Winnicott wrote, the mother 'adapts less and less completely, gradually, according to the infant's growing ability to deal with her failure' (Winnicott, 1953). Good parents bond, love and then start to let go over time. If they don't, the child can never become her or his own self.

Winnicott wrote relatively little about fathers but did stress they had to give mother and child emotional support. I have adapted some of his ideas to develop the concept of the good enough father.

The good enough father also is not perfect. But he tries, he is present and he does not commit the terrible sins – being abusive to his children, denying them emotional warmth, ignoring and just not caring for them. None of this is rocket science though it may require you to make peace with difficult unresolved feelings you may have about how you were fathered. Anthony Astrachan in *How Men Feel* (1978) argued one reason many men were ambivalent and often cold fathers was that their own fathers taught them nothing about being a father.

Self Analysis 1
Ask yourself:
What are your best memories of your father?
Are you condemned to repeat history if the memories are not good?
What might help you get over it?

The Ten Commandments for Parents

One of the pleasures of writing a book is ferreting out long-forgotten sources. In 1979, a German professor of comparative education, Leonhard Froeze of the University of Marburg, wrote *Ten Commandments for Adults* and especially for parents. They seem to me utterly sensible. They are:

Thou shalt regard the child as the highest good entrusted to you.
Thou shalt not form the child in thine own image.
Children need free space for the unfolding of their physical and spiritual powers.
Thou shalt respect the child's personality.
Thou shalt not use force against the child.
Thou shalt not destroy the confidence of the child.
Thou shalt protect the child against death.
Thou shalt not tempt the child to lie.
Thou shalt recognise the child's needs.
Thou shalt give the child his and her rights.

The basic rule is to realise how much children need parents. It is simple to say that but we often fail children – and so does society.

Children in trouble

A total of 100,000 children run away from home every year, a quarter being under 14, according to The Children's Society. As if that is not bad enough, Britain locks up more children under 16 than any country in Europe. Sir David Ramsbotham, who was Inspector of Prisons, repeatedly complained about the dreadful facilities for children in prisons every year till in 2005 he handed over to Anne Owers. Every year since then, she has issued similar warnings. The Children's Society also complains that 11,000 children under 16 are sent to prison every year.

In 2006, Parliament appointed a Commissioner for Children. Two years later, he delivered a shattering attack on the suffering inflicted in detention centres on children of asylum seekers. These very vulnerable children were being mistreated and the Home Office (the British Ministry of the Interior) clearly did not care.

In the wake of the death of Baby P in Haringey which dominated the headlines in the winter of 2008, there have been claims that one in ten children in well-off countries like Britain suffer some kind of abuse (*The Lancet*, December 2008). The number of children who suffer from mental health problems is also increasing; more and more of them are being treated on adult psychiatric wards. Vulnerable children don't get the specialist help they need.

Do we love and respect our children? Of course we do. The government even has a Minister for Children. I asked the Department of Children for a comment on the Ten Commandments for Parents and was told I had got it wrong. The only Ten Commandments were those in the Bible.

3

Fathers have a history

Being a father today is – and is not – like being a father at other times. Since I have quoted *Ten Commandments for Parents* it's only fair to quote the one older commandment for children:

'Honour thy mother and thy father that thy days may be long on the land that the Lord thy God has given thee,' says the 6th Commandment.

Honouring mum and dad is not so easy these days especially in the West where the traditional family is in confusion, divorce is frequent and millions of us live in stepfamilies or, to use today's sociological jargon, 'blended families'. Blended whiskies tend to be blander than pure malts but this is not true of blended families. They can be good but also they can be toxic.

A Young Minds report in August 2008 claimed that one third of teenagers in Britain have virtually no contact with their parents. These teens were not in care but in the ordinary course of life, they had virtually nothing to do with mum and dad. They lived in the same house, took food out of the same fridge but didn't speak a word to each other.

Very Pinter-esque. The silence of the family. The silence in the family.

Silence is, alas, not the most destructive tragedy. In 2002, Holly Wells and Jessica Chapman went missing in Soham. The story dominated the headlines. I made a film *Our Daughter Holly* with the parents of Holly Wells. Kevin and Nicola Wells told me how they were amazed – and furious – when they realised the police considered them suspects. They endured a three-hour search of their house – 'every piece of furniture was lifted with military precision'. It was only after the police were sure the Wells had nothing to do with the disappearance of the children that they began to take them into their confidence. The Wells family was distressed but there are reasons why the first instinct of the police is to look at the family. The tragedies come from every country.

In 2009 in Austria, Josef Fritzl (who had links with neo Nazi parties) was found guilty of abusing his daughter and killing one other child. Earlier Fritzl had shown investigators round the cellar where he kept his eldest daughter, Elisabeth, for 24 years, fathering seven children on her. But Fritzl wasn't that bad, his lawyers insisted. He had installed an electronic timer that could unlock the door in case of an emergency. Austrian police believe he was even lying about that as the door was usually sealed off with metal bars.

In the autumn of 2008, Britain saw a series of tragedies. First, a failed businessman Christopher Forster shot his 15-year-old daughter as well as her mother. The police suggested he could not bring himself to tell his wife and daughter he had lost all his money. A few weeks later news of the death of Baby P became public. An inquiry showed that Haringey social services had visited the baby's filthy home 60 times and that doctors had often seen the child but no professional saw Baby P was being viciously abused. We now know that Baby P had a four-year-old sibling who was being raped by her stepfather. A week after the Baby P case hit the headlines came news of a trial in Sheffield where a father was found guilty of raping his daughters for over eight years. In between a fireman killed his two children.

There are some 15,000 children on the at risk register in Britain at any one time. Corby (2000) found that between 7 per cent and 29 per cent of women in different countries claimed to have been abused as children. Reported cases of child abuse in the United States have risen from 400,000 in the 1970s to almost three million a year. Fifty-two per cent of the victims suffer emotional neglect, 25 per cent physical abuse, 13 per cent suffer sexual abuse. Fathers and step-fathers commit much of the abuse.

The latest statistics on domestic violence while women are pregnant are also shocking. In Ireland, 12.9 per cent of women at an antenatal clinic had suffered 'intimate partner abuse'; in India, 18 per cent of women in a sample of 2,199 reported domestic violence during their last pregnancy; in England, a study of 475 pregnant women reported that 17 per cent of them had suffered violence against their persons (Cook and Bewley, 2008). Drink often played a part in the violence.

The ultimate tragedies are murders. Margo Wilson and Martin Daly of McMaster University studied 239 cases of 'family wipe-out', where men kill their wives and children. Men kill, they concluded, because the women are too inde-pendent. 'If I can't have her, then nobody can,' is how the men think. Such jealousy often also condemns children to death. In other species, fathers rarely kill their offspring. The only species as cruel to its young as we are is the hyena. Inspiring!

Why do fathers abuse children?

The excuses men give for abusing women and children usually involve stress and how their own parents treated them. In 1991, National Children's Home claimed one third of child abusers had been abused as children themselves. I made a film *The Last Taboo* for Channel 4 about this research. One abuser told me his father had started 'playing with my willy when we had baths together'. His father had also loaned him out to 'mates' to abuse. By the time he was 12, Ray said he was abusing younger children. It does not take mathematical sophistication to realise that it's a poor excuse. If one third of abusers have themselves been abused, two thirds of children who have been abused do not become abusers. History does not have to repeat itself.

As men, we have choices – and we must choose to protect children. I do not believe the extreme feminist view that all men are inherently violent is helpful. Most men are not. I want to suggest one other cause of abuse which has not been much studied yet.

Some violent men see their victims just as objects; in other cases, the men are the very opposite of this cold objective menace. Some dramatic cases of 'family wipe-out syndrome' suggest violent men often have a very poor sense of boundaries (Palermo and Ross, 1999). This would make some acts of violence against children not acts of callous hatred but, paradoxically, partly the result of men being more involved with their children. The men don't have the emotional skills to cope with their own feelings if they lose their jobs, their woman has an affair or their children defy them. They persuade themselves they are victims and 'console' themselves by abusing, and sometimes killing their children. Sometimes such men claim to be protecting the children because life is so difficult.

It should be said that mothers who have been abused are also likely to abuse their own children; abused girls live with and marry violent men more than average.

In Kathmandu – more blood than at the end of Hamlet

Given how fathers treat children, there are inevitably cases of revenge – and one of them took place in Nepal. As we shall see it is bizarre that this small remote country has seen two important and very dramatic events linked to the subject of this book.

In Kathmandu Palace on 1 June 2001, Prince Dipendra handed drinks to his family; a few minutes later he came back with a machine gun. He then shot the King, his father, and nine other relatives. The last thing the King said to his son was that he should come back properly dressed. You did not serve cocktails in combat gear. The domineering dad and the son who finally spews out his revenge. Freud would have recognised the dynamic because he had written a truly weird book about fathers and sons.

In his bizarre *Totem and Taboo* (1913), Freud argued that one of the key events in history, deep in the Stone Age, was the revolt of the sons. Readers must now imagine they are in the Primeval Jungle-ville in the territory of the ancient tribe I will frivolously call the Hormones.

The sons of Hormone lust for the women in the tribe. But the old Hormones have the power and the clubs. Lust crazed, the young men murder all the fathers and pounce on all the women. The dreams of his middle-class patients in Vienna revealed just such Neanderthal passions, Freud believed. There was never such a jungle as that city in the early 1900s.

Once they'd done in the dads, the Hormone brothers felt guilty. So they set up the dead father as a totem. Father Hormone could now be worshipped. Freud liked things to be complex – pun intended – so the guilty sons also had to punish themselves.

You can imagine them scratching their Neanderthal heads and wondering how to do that. Then, the Stone Age son with a conscience had an idea. The light bulb lit up over his head. Eu-bloody-reka, he thought, centuries before the Greeks. It would make them feel better if they gave something up and he suggested the supreme sacrifice; they would not sleep with their mothers. This was the origin of the incest taboo, Freud argued.

I did stress *Totem and Taboo* was bizarre. It is a wonderful fable. Then there is the Bible which has many inspiring examples of how fathers love their children – and some very rum ones. Jews, Muslims and Christians revere the patriarch Abraham but if he were alive today, he'd be reported to social services.

In Genesis the Lord tells Abraham to take his son Isaac to the top of the Mount Moriah; Isaac is to be sacrificed but the lad doesn't know it. Does Abraham tell the Lord not to break one of his own soon-to-be-published Ten Commandments 'Thou Shalt Not Kill' or, simply, 'Beg pardon, Jehovah, family comes first. And what am I going to tell the wife? She's very fond of the boy as she managed, thanks to You, to have him when she was 100 years old?'

The answer is none of the above. When Isaac asks why they are not taking a lamb to sacrifice with them up the mountain, Abraham does not tell his son the truth. The

Lord will provide the sacrifice, Abraham stalls. He fails to mention to Isaac his starring role in the sacrifice scenario. Then Abraham ties poor Isaac down on the altar. Tension mounts; Isaac trembles. The kid's no fool; dad is sharpening his knife. Then . . .

Out of the blue, it's the miracle moment.

Enter the ram whose horns just happened to have been caught in a thicket. Exit the ram soon after, roasted with 'sweet smelling herbs pleasing to the Lord'. So the Almighty has roast ram and Isaac does not end up as well dead as well as well seasoned. *Genesis* does not explore what effect the drama had on the future relationship between Abraham and his son. This does not feel realistic to me. I get into trouble if I tell my younger son he shouldn't smoke or drink so much.

One author who had insight into the ambivalence of fathers was the sixteenth-century Frenchman, Michel de Montaigne. He pointed out that 'very often we are more moved by our children's frolickings, games and infantile nonsense than by their mature acts. It is as if we loved them for our amusement, as monkeys, not as human beings.'

Too often fathers acted mean and distant to keep their children 'in awe and obedience. This is the most futile farce,' Montaigne said. It could end in tragedy as in the case of The Marechal de Monluc, a friend of Montaigne's. Monluc's son was brave, but he never learned what his father really felt for him. Monluc confessed to Montaigne that he was grief stricken because he never told his son how much he loved him and his son died young. The boy only saw his father as a grim man with a grim frown and died 'thinking I could neither love him nor value him,' Monluc mourned. Montaigne warned other fathers not to be so short-sighted.

In the eighteenth century some fathers started to keep diaries in which they noted how children developed – and what philosophical conclusions you could draw from that. You don't have to be so intellectual but a diary is a good idea. It will allow you to remember the milestones – and the problems – better. It's also a good way of getting rid of frustrations. Writing can be a form of therapy.

Self Analysis 2
Consider keeping a diary of your baby's progress.
What would be the high points?
What would be the moments of fear?
When would you show it to your child?

Even great generals could be sentimental fathers. In 1852, *Punch* printed an obituary on the Duke of Wellington, who beat Napoleon at the battle of Waterloo. The Duke was nearly as good a father as an Emperor penguin. The obituary said:

> That underneath the armour of his breast
> Were springs of tenderness – all quick to flow.
> In sympathy with childhood's joy or woe:
> That children climbed his knees, and made his arms their nest.
>
> ('Wellington', *Punch*, 1852, p. 135)

But the pundit's view was more acid. Claudia Nelson has studied how fathers were depicted in magazines between 1850 and 1910. Many writers saw fathers as ineffectual or uninvolved; many suggested it would be wise to keep them away from the nursery because men were 'mere amateurs of the home' (Nelson, 2007).

By the 1920s, the new science of psychology offered often insecure mothers and fathers advice.

Scientific fathering

One of the first scientific experts on parenting was John B. Watson (1878–1958), the founder of the psychological school known as behaviourism. He was born in Greenville, North Carolina, in 1878. His own delinquent father, Pickens, ran away from home to canoodle with a Native American woman when John was ten. The boy was devastated but recovered quite quickly, as he had a warm mother and a loving nanny; he was resourceful and got to university. But he remained insecure. Watson found it hard to sleep in the dark and had to have a night light on for much of his life. With such a childhood Watson was almost bound to become an expert on parenting.

Watson wrote a book with his second wife, Rosalie Rayner. *The Psychological Care of the Infant and Child* (Watson and Watson, 1929) argued fathers had to restrain the appalling behaviour of mothers. Mothers were too soft and kept on smothering baby with hugs and kisses. Most mothers, Watson said were guilty of '*psychological* murder . . . I know hundreds who want to possess their children's souls.' Watson outraged 1920s women's groups, complaining 'kissing the baby to death is just about as popular a sport as it has ever been'. Once when he and his wife went on a drive with friends, he noticed the mother kissed her baby 32 times. Watson shocked the Mothers Union even more by suggesting that all this kissing 'is at bottom a sex seeking response'.

Fathers had to protect babies from such smother love but, unfortunately, many were more obsessed with getting their children to obey them. 'Most fathers should be punished for the idiotic parental duty dogma they try to instil in their young.' The duty dogma was that children owed their parents. 'Children don't owe their parents anything,' Watson countered. He had cause to be bitter himself. His own father, who had abandoned him and his mother, started to turn up at his office when Watson became rich. Did remorseful Dad want to see his son? Not really. He realised that he could touch his boy for 10 or 20 dollars – which Pickens used to get pickled.

I wrote a biography of Watson and visited his daughter and one of his sons. James (who had become an industrial psychologist) told me he thought his father was influenced by Freud. A child who was touched too much by his mother might fall in love with her and Freud suggested being too close to one's mother might make a man homosexual. So Watson kept his physical distance. 'I respected my father as a man but not as a father really,' James told me. When his mother died, he felt the lack of affection at home very badly. But Watson had faith in children and thought they could talk about problems with their parents. A well run family sat down and discussed what we now call 'issues'. Children could talk about difficult matters sensibly. Good enough fathering for Watson meant rational but cool father. He spent far more time with his children than most men.

Ironically Watson has recently been attacked by Desmond Morris, author of *The Naked Man* (Morris, 2008). Unjustly Morris accuses Watson of wanting to turn children into replicas of their fathers. In fact, Watson wanted children to be their own independent selves as young as they could.

Real men aren't fathers

Before the 1980s, if fathers spent much time on childcare, it was nearly always due to economic circumstances. Men were unemployed and women had to become the bread-winner. In Lancashire, they sneered at men on the dole who were forced to look after the children and called them 'Mary Annes'. And men weren't very good at it anyway.

In 1952, *The Times* published one of its amusing short editorials which poked fun at a father who takes his children to a party. Dad's first problem is how to deal with 'the continuous din of tin whistles, mouth organs and hooters punctuated by the bursting of balloons, each explosion being followed by a wail of grief or rage'. This is too much for the poor man. When he has to talk about his kids, he has no idea what to say; he knows very little about them. When he has to leave, his hostess has to 'tell him who his children are in case he does not recognise them'. *The Times* did not ask what effect Dad's pathetic behaviour would have on them. Would his daughters think what a twit!?

Fifty years later, the issues were not that different in Manhattan. When Woody Allen split from Mia Farrow, he wanted custody of his adopted son, Moses, but the funny man's fathering skills did not impress the judge. The judge commented that Woody did not often dress his children or give them baths. The director of *Annie Hall* did not know the name of Moses' teachers or of his dentist. Woody knew little about how well Moses was doing at school.

I now go from comic royalty to historical royalty.

One justification for the British monarchy is that it sets a good example to 'ordinary people'. But Britain's royal family does not seem to have had any spectacularly successful father–son relationships for the last 150 years.

Prince Albert was a stern father. One of his sons ended up involved in a case about cheating at cards.

Edward VIII was regarded by his father George V as a bad lot. King George thought his younger son pathetic as he stammered.

George VI doted on both daughters, especially on Elizabeth who became the Queen. It has to be said, however, that the late Princess Margaret seems to have always been rather a desperate seeker for love. The recent biography of her first husband Lord Snowdon (De Courcey, 2008) paints Margaret as a woman who was always seeking the love of men. Did George VI pay more attention to Elizabeth knowing that she would succeed him on the throne and did Margaret pay the price for that?

Prince Philip on his eightieth birthday said that he didn't think his son Charles would make much of a king. Thanks Dad. After the massacre in Nepal, a cartoon in the *Evening Standard* showed the Queen and Prince Philip wandering around Buckingham Palace in bullet proof vests . . . just in case Prince Charles dreamed of imitating the actions of Prince Dipendra – the psychotic family killer.

Fathers keep out

Sometimes the literature makes you feel dads will always be in the doghouse. Rosalind Miles heads her chapter on the Father Almighty with Joe Orton's snappy, 'It's all that any reasonable child can expect if the dad is present at the conception.' Is that brilliant quote from a brilliant 'queer', as Orton called himself, really the last word on what all men feel about being fathers? I would say not but if you argue men should be more involved, you can get unexpected flak.

Writing on Father's Day 1985 in *The Observer*, I pleaded for men to take on more chores and childcare and enjoy the pleasures of fatherhood. I wasn't suggesting I was a saint, but I didn't expect to be attacked. No less a writer than Katherine Whitehorn wrote a counter-piece arguing that I wanted to deprive women of the one area of life where they were in charge.

It would be wrong to end on a down note, however. In 1798 William Wordsworth wrote a sweet poem about his son:

> I have a boy of five years old;
> His face is fair and fresh to see;
> His limbs are cast in beauty's mould,
> and dearly he loves me.
>
> One morn we strolled on our dry walk,
> Our quiet home all full in view,
> And held such intermitted talk
> As we are wont to do.

Wordsworth got it right. Walk, talk, play with your kids, cuddle them. It's not rocket science.

One very positive feature of the first decade of the twenty-first century has been the rise of the celebrity dad. Brad Pitt and David Beckham have been good examples of that. Both have been very public about how much they enjoy being fathers.

New York Times reporter David Carr in his *The Night of the Gun* (2008) even claims his daughters helped him recover from alcoholism when he had to look after them. 'I had no idea what I was doing but children teach you how to care for them. Leave the house without an extra diaper and they will have some brutal smelly event at a McDonald's.' Carr says that as he came to know his twins better, he came to adore them and devised a song about being 'the nicest girls in town'. His lyrics won't win prizes but the sentiment is lovely.

> They are so nice, they are so sweet
> I love them twice, they can't be beat.

But it takes time for many men to realise that.

4

The only true immortality
– for a man

My late mother-in-law, Aileen Blong La Tourette, told me once that children were the only true immortality. A woman who is giving you a child, an incomparable gift, should be treated with love and respect. In your dreams, some women might say.

Learning you are going to become a father should be a simple joy, but often it is not. Many men do feel triumphant when they find out they are going to be a dad, but others feel anxious and afraid, afraid for what they are about to lose and afraid because of the responsibility. It's again an area that has been rather little researched. A recent piece of self analysis is very illuminating though.

In his blog at *Irony Central*, the American Jeff Vogel catches the mood of many prospective but worried fathers well. Vogel writes very honestly; 'I am having a very hard time being happy about it. The closer it gets to the birth day, the harder it is for me to look at an infant without wincing . . . I believe that anyone who has the right to have the child also has the right to be unhappy about how much it is going to suck.' Vogel's feelings 'are a subtle mix of terror and horror'. But when he tells people that, 'I tend to get a shocked, offended look.'

Vogel argues his feelings are rational.

I am about to have to care for a frail, helpless infant life. Read any baby book. Read the lists of warnings and missteps, any of which will treat your infant to a speedy, horrible death. You aren't supposed to let a small baby sleep with sheets on it, because they might STRANGLE IT.

Source: www.CartoonStock.com

Even if you haven't read any books, if the prospect of being a new parent looking after a helpless baby does not fill you with at least a small measure of terror, I'm sorry. There is something wrong with you. And as for the fulfilling part, I'm sorry. I suppose I buy it on some theoretical level, like quantum tunnelling and black holes. But the good things about being a parent are very theoretical and intangible, and the bad things are very real and imminent. I have no idea what it feels like to have my child look up at me and smile, or to hear her talk for the first time, or to see her graduate from college. I have no idea what those things feel like.

On the other hand, I know exactly what it is like to not sleep. I am very familiar with what it feels like to worry. And, while I have not personally experienced being up to my elbows in shit and vomit, I can vividly imagine it. And I know what it is like to worry that someone I love will die.

I'm not uncaring. I will love my child. That's what makes it so terrifying. If I didn't care about my unborn daughter so much, I wouldn't be so afraid. I'm not irrational. The risks are real. The costs are real. I'm not making any of this stuff up.

Vogel rings so true and, typically, says nothing about his own father. Most fathers-to-be are unlikely to find out about how to behave from their own fathers because father–son relations tend to avoid such intimacies. Blendis (1988) asked men how they felt about their own fathers. Did they remember a warm or a distant relationship? Her sample was small – 31 men in her first study and 119 in her second one. Of the first 31, only three had truly positive memories. Of the second sample, only around 28 reported good relationships with their fathers. No one said their father had helped prepare them for being a father.

When I became a father, my own father gave me two pieces of advice only. First, 'you have to honour the mother of your children'. Second, 'make sure they go to a decent school'. I'm not sure he was so reticent because he felt bad he had abandoned me.

Even the usually progressive Scandinavians have problems when they become fathers. In Norway, many complain they are now out in the snow, as it were, exiled to the margins of their families the moment the first child is born. The best Norwegian dad can do is help out when the mother needs a rest from breastfeeding. But some men also face a problem they don't like to talk about.

I am Peter Pan – men who fear growing up

Jane was 27 years old and was married to an accountant whose real passion was playing football. She wanted to have a child but he kept on saying he was not ready, the figure skater, my nickname for accountants, didn't see how he could concentrate on sport if he had to be a dad. Jane's biological clock was ticking away. The conflict lasted some years; the marriage didn't.

snap back at her and remember you owe it to her as she is carrying your child to make a big effort.

Here are some possible ways of coping with mood swings. Do your best to understand what is going on. Secondly, tenderness and humour help. Be tender towards her and wry about the situation. Ask:

Are you fed up or is the baby being grumpy?

And be playful. Ask:

What do you think the baby is thinking?

The baby, of course, is not yet thinking as she or he is in the womb, but it may help to lift the mood or switch the focus.

I have developed a silly game which can help with some mood swings.

You sit in bed with your partner, you extend your arms above your head, then you say loudly 'Hold horns high.' The phrase comes from a science fiction novel by Brian Aldiss in which humans and bird-like creatures called phagors compete to rule the planet Heliconia. The phagors are always telling each other to hold horns high. We may not have horns but we can pretend. It is hard to feel utterly depressed with your arms held up.

My game is completely ridiculous, but being ridiculous is an excellent way of defusing stress.

There are less loopy ways of helping. Let the mum-to-be rest when she needs to. Offer plenty of cuddles and talk about your plans for the baby. Make sure she eats well as she is eating for two. Indulge whatever weird cravings she may have while making sure that she gets a good diet with plenty of whole grain breads and fruit and vegetables.

If you like watching *House* you will know that most flats or houses contain dangerous household products. Dr House is always sending his medics to break into the homes of patients to find Chemical X which is killing them. So learn the House lesson. Don't let your partner near paint thinner, solvents, pesticides and, probably, the cat's litter box.

The National Childbirth Trust now offers detailed information in leaflets and has even set up an online support group to give dads an opportunity to share their anxieties with other fathers-to-be.

Sex, drink and smoking

Smoking harms the baby in the womb. Children whose mothers smoke are born smaller and their brains are also smaller. The evidence is so strong that if the mother does not want to give up smoking the man should do his best to persuade her to do so. That can be rough for both of you, but the evidence of the harm smoking does to the baby in the womb is impossible to argue with. It is no good fathers-to-be expecting the mother to give up if they don't, so you also need to give up smoking as exposure to smoke harms the baby. You will also have to help the mother through the withdrawal changes. Fun!

The risks of drinking are more debated. Excessive drinking is clearly damaging but guidelines put out in 2008 suggest moderate drinking does not harm. My banker friend Alex gave up drinking when his Lithuanian wife Asta did so. I admire his will power. A year later, his complexion is rather more baby-like than it was. Abstinence makes you glow!

There's usually no medical need to give up sex, though Rosemary Miles suggests many women do not want to have sex while they are pregnant. They see their body as theirs and the child's. Dads should keep out. The mystery of hormones can cut it both ways. Sometimes pregnancy makes women far randier as their bodies are awash with hormones.

It is one of those times when, absolutely, what the woman wants goes. Nagging your pregnant wife, or partner, to have sex when she doesn't want to, is storing up trouble. And trouble can have odd consequences. A woman's fear of vaginal delivery is strongly associated with her dissatisfaction with the couple relationship (Saisto *et al.*, 2001). This in an intriguing finding especially given that Caesarean births have risen steeply in recent years. Some statistics now claim

www.babycentre.co.uk and that of The National Childbirth Trust encourage mothers-to-be and their partners to think about labour and the birth of the baby. The issues are basic but vital:

where the mother will have the baby
who she wants to be with her at the birth
what will make her feel more comfortable
what kind of pain relief to ask for
what mother and father should do in the baby's first hours
how to feed your baby.

Making her feel special as a woman

Some women glow during pregnancy; others become anxious and moody. There are simple things men can do to help.

Make the mother feel loved and special. Presents can help. Giving flowers has almost never been known to harm a relationship. It is also nice to give the mother (who may by now feel like a balloon) something feminine and romantic. You may not be able to afford a bottle of Chanel No. 5 or Dior but Body Shop do a nice range of cheap-ish scents. The thought counts.

Being pregnant can get boring so also make sure your partner has some good books to read – and not just books about being how to be a mum.

If you can afford it, take her out to dinner. If not, get a take away. If you can't spend the money on that, cook her something you know she likes.

In these tough economic times, you do not have to buy everything. There is no shame in asking family and friends if you can borrow a cot, changing table, toys and baby clothes. I've often got amazing stuff in charity shops – and I have browsed them both when I've been hard up and when I've been flush.

And finally, count your blessings – and not just the obvious ones. While you wait for the baby to be born, be glad you're not living in Greece 30 years ago. We spent four months there when Aileen was pregnant with our second child. Everyone was appalled by the fact that she went swimming in the sea and had baths. Didn't we know? Water could harm the baby in the womb. For a woman to smell like an old goat who never used deodorant was a small price to pay for giving birth to a healthy baby. It should be stressed that there is absolutely no evidence that pregnant women don't have to wash. In fact being soaped by the father of your child-to-be can be nicely intimate.

5

In at the birth

To the day I die, I will never forget the birth of either of my children. I am glad to say that in being present when Nicholas was born in Greenwich hospital and when Reuben was born in our flat, I was acting very scientifically.

The research could not be more in favour of fathers being in at the birth. Gibbins and Thomson (2001) found women benefit when they feel 'in control' of the birth process. Getting support from their partner during the birth is associated with that as well as with a quicker delivery and with less pain. Being there also helps fathers as they are likely to be more involved with their children.

When Nicholas was born, I had been to a few antenatal classes but nothing prepared me for either the tension or the joy. Aileen was given an injection of pethidine which slowed down the birth. For about 15 minutes, while Nicholas was stuck in the birth canal, I heard voices in my head. I prayed to God that he would be born healthy and without brain damage. My inner voice replied. Yes, he would be safe but he would also be born speaking – and carrying an important message from God to Greenwich SE10. Out of the mouth of the babe Jehovah would speak.

I managed to keep news of the forthcoming divine message to myself, so I was not taken to the psychiatric ward. My friend Keesup went through a worse ordeal 25 years later. His wife was scheduled to have a Caesarean. Then, because she was dilated, the doctors changed their minds and decided she could give birth naturally. Then, they gave her pethidine as the baby was not pointed the right way. As had happened to Aileen the drugs slowed down the delivery. It took an agonising eight hours for Scherezade to be born. When I told Keesup of our experiences in Greenwich, we concluded obstetricians seem to know less than they think.

Dads need to be ready to ask questions of doctors. Here are some obvious ones:

What stage of labour do you think we are at?
Are there any problems you can see?
Just why are you proposing to give drugs?
What will the effect of those drugs be?

The most important thing is to insist the mother is told exactly what is going on and to ask doctors and midwives to explain what they are doing. Not easy during an exciting but tense time.

Some writers suggest men can't take being in at the birth and that a stressed birth partner hardly helps: stress, like fear, can contaminate. Maternal stress can slow down labour so that fathers' stress levels are often very high at key points during the birthing process (Johnson, 2002; Henneborn and Cogan, 1975).

Men, have no doubts. This will be the only time I offer myself as a role model. If I can manage being in at the birth, you can do it. I am squeamish, comically squeamish. I once made a film about eyes and I could not watch two minutes of it when it was being shot or edited.

Your baby's worth it. Your woman's worth it. You're worth it. Studies show high levels of satisfaction post partum for both mothers and fathers who shared the experience of labour and birth (Chan and Paterson-Brown, 2002).

Given Keesup's experiences, it is telling one study shows that the presence of the father can help compensate for poor quality obstetric services. Twenty years ago obstetricians greatly underestimated the psychological boost fathers give to their partners during delivery – as well as the practical support the men provide during labour, and afterwards (Hayward and Chalmers, 1990). This study has

Source: www.CartoonStock.com

not been repeated since as far as I can tell but Keesup's experiences suggest it is still true.

Fathers are five times more likely to touch their partner during labour and delivery than any other friend or 'supporter' who is there (Klein *et al.*, 1981). So it's a good thing 97 per cent dads are in there rather than pacing outside and smoking a fag in the waiting room. If you smoke in a hospital these days, you probably get beheaded at once.

It used to be thought that a dad who attended the birth would fancy the mother of his children less. No serious research supports this fable of men who are put off forever by the biological realities (Odent, 1999). Except in Newfoundland perhaps. There levels of the male hormone testosterone drop by up to 33 per cent in new fathers. The sample was very small, however, as I said before, just 31 men (Delahunty *et al.*, 2007). Sadly she does not say how long it takes for the hormone to return to normal levels.

There is a significant correlation between fathers being present at the birth and infant health. Fathers who went to the birth participated more in 'well child visits' (Moore and Kotelchuck, 2004). Recent research from China shows a strong correlation between how much practical support the father gave and how long he spent with the mother during labour (Ip, 2000).

The better relationship, the better the parenting

The findings all point in one direction. Women who have the full support of their partners bond more closely to their children, and are more responsive and sensitive to their needs (Feiring, 1976). This is true of teenage mothers, too (Mercer *et al.*, 1984). The quality of the relationship between the parents predicts how both mother and father nurture and respond to their children's needs (Guterman and Lee, 2005).

This book both is – and is not – scientific and I believe it is useful for men to read about the experiences of other men when they became fathers. Given the success of celebrity books, I am surprised we still don't have many celebrity dad memoirs. A book of celeb interviews on what being a dad means to me – with contributions by Beckham, Blair, Brad Pitt – would probably do rather well.

After Nicholas was born and Aileen was sleeping, I ran up the steep hill from Greenwich hospital to our flat. I don't think I have ever been so high. I rang my mother, Aileen's parents, and my father to tell them the good news. The only other time I've been so simply, totally happy was when Reuben was born. It was not just because I had become a dad but because, with both my children, I had been there during the whole process from the breaking of the waters to the first breath.

Touch matters

My friend David Carr Brown was also present at the birth of his first daughter in Paris. 'It was a pretty tough labour and about two hours before she gave birth, my wife literally fainted.' In his teens David had been a hospital porter in Guildford and 'so I had been around such scenes. In addition, the baby was pointing the wrong way. Her feet were coming out first.' David now remembered his early career and started helping the nurse. 'She was pulling on the feet and I was helping push the baby out.'

He's always been admirably practical. But also touching.

'When my daughter Alexandra was born, the nurse gave her to me to hold because I was there,' David told me.

David's second child was born nine years later. By then he had left his wife and met Murielle. She did not find out she was pregnant until she was four months 'with child'. 'The French pride themselves on their medical services but one day she got a letter from the hospital, where she'd gone for something else. The letter said that we are very sorry but, when you came here, we failed to notice the fact that you are pregnant.' It continued to be a dramatic pregnancy.

About four months later, David was filming in Italy. The baby was not due for another month. He got a phone call saying Murielle was in labour unexpectedly early. 'I got the night train and I made it in time. I was there two hours before the birth but she didn't want me to be present. Partly that was because we really didn't know each other that well, and partly because she had to have a Caesarean.'

When Murielle had their second child, however, David was at the birth. 'It was the first time I had deliberately set out to have a child,' he told me. For him what had changed most over time was the attitude of the nurses. 'They assumed I knew nothing and when Julian was born they gave him to me to hold, saying it'll be good for you to do that. I suppose I am unusual in that with two of my three children, I held them before their mother did.'

Memories are made of this

The poet T.S. Eliot wrote about the night with the photograph album. Your baby will be a newborn only for a short time. Keep a record. Take pictures, take videos. It does not matter if you are at home or in hospital. They will be very precious.

Andy noticed changes during the first 17 days of his daughter's life. 'Grace is a very laid-back baby at 17 days.

She eats and she sleeps. She's just beginning to take notice of things, just beginning to smile.' Just 17 days old – and already developing. It was very sweet to hear Andy talk just like a man in love. Fathers now have to find out just who is this little human they are starting to love.

And that love should be practical.

Bringing baby home

Bringing the baby home is exciting but also stressful. Fathers have to accept they are the least important person for now. Now is the time to take over the cleaning, the laundry and the cooking. Now is the time to make your love practical. If you don't, you may find it being flung back in your face later on. Not doing your share may well lead to anger and resentment.

Who changes the nappies?

Whose job is it to see the baby is clean?

Who gets up in the middle of the night when she's howling?

Women can lose out in terms of their careers because they are stuck with the childcare. Superwoman may manage to cook, look after the kids and operate at the level she worked at before she had children, but why should women be forced to be superwomen – and usually when Superwoman is interviewed it turns out she has nannies. Anna Wintour, the editor of *Vogue*, on whom Meryl Streep's character in *The Devil Wears Prada* is apparently not based, is said to get up every morning at 6 a.m. to have quality time with her children. Most women can't afford nannies so it's the bloke who needs to step up.

Be willing to negotiate with your wife or partner. But do it with more generosity than at any other time in your life. She has borne that baby for the two of you.

Baby love – jealousy sucks . . .

Don't forget in the middle of what will be hard work to enjoy your new baby. Talk to him or her. Share the care. In

Britain paternity leave is a mere two weeks. Try to save up holiday time so you can spend more time at home helping.

There are also psychological issues. The new mother is likely to give her new baby, her new love, total attention. Many men admit they feel jealous. Blendis (1988) found some evidence of this, but it would be nice to have more research. The absence of precise research is surprising. 'Often, after a baby is born, the focus is on the mum, but dads have needs too as their identity changes and we are helping to address this,' according to a statement by the chief executive of the National Childbirth Trust (2007).

Again an odd, telling finding; when a father takes frequent care of a firstborn, the child shows more positive behaviours toward the mother, after the birth of a second sibling (Kojima *et al.*, 2001).

Most mothers adore their babies and, once they have recovered from the tiredness of pregnancy, enjoy mothering. But a small percentage can't cope, don't like it and do not bond with their babies. Some 15 per cent of mothers develop postnatal depression, a serious problem which needs serious and sensitive attention.

Unfortunately, most GPs treat postnatal depression with tranquillisers and/or antidepressants and not much else. In 2006, 31 million prescriptions were written for such drugs – one for every two people in the UK. Yet the warnings about too much reliance on such drugs are now very ancient. David Healy, professor of psychiatry at Cardiff, has warned that antidepressants give too few benefits and have too many side effects (Healy, 2004). Professor Irving Kirsch of Hull University has warned: 'there seems little evidence to support the prescription of anti-depressant medication to any but the most severely depressed patients, unless alternative treatments have failed to provide benefit.' Kirsch reached his conclusion after studying 35 clinical trials, involving more than 5,000 patients. In most cases, the mental health of those taking antidepressants improved little more than those on placebos.

If the mother of your newborn is not just tired but getting depressed, talk to her, go with her to the doctor. Fathers should always have phone numbers for the GP in case of any emergency. While listening to medical advice do everything you can to persuade her not just to rely on antidepressants if that is all the doctor offers. Antidepressants can work well in the short term, but they have side effects and they can not replace talking about why the new mother is unhappy. Many people get addicted to antidepressants as they are hard to give up, as hard as hard drugs are.

One thing you can do is make sure you are not increasing your partner's depression because she is always exhausted.

Go to sleep you little creep

Often the most immediate problem is sleep. The baby doesn't sleep properly so mum does not get her shut-eye. Research at the University of San Diego in 2008 found that 32 per cent of mothers said they did not get anything like enough sleep.

Getting up in the middle of the night to feed your baby is an excellent way of bonding with him or her. If the mother is breastfeeding, you can still be the one who gets up, picks baby up and bring him or her to bed, so that the mother is not alone while she feeds. If the baby is being part breast part bottle fed, one of the most sensible times for giving the baby a bottle is in the middle of the night. Fathers can do that.

A baby can be very exhausting. We used to have a rocking chair and that was a mistake. For a time, Nicholas only fell asleep while being rocked. You really can't do much else while rocking a baby. You can't even watch TV. Luckily, twenty-first-century technology offers help.

Play your favourite music while you are feeding the baby in the middle of the night. If you don't want to wake the mother or the neighbours, wear headphones.

There is the perfect image of twenty-first-century dad – feeding his baby at 3 a.m. wearing headphones listening to *Chicago*, Bach or whatever makes you feel good.

One of the things I did was to make up silly lullabies.

Go to sleep
Go to sleep
Don't make me weep
You little creep.

The last line was often sung with great feeling!

Fathers also need to be prepared for something women have known for centuries. Looking after kids is not always fun. Charlie Lewis suggested men devote more time to playing with their children because playing is more fun and less work. An unflattering picture! This not an isolated finding about British men.

In Norway Storo and Jansen (2006) also found fathers spend a great deal of time playing with their children rather than in more practical childcare. The reason I'm afraid does not require in depth research. It is more fun playing peek-a-boo with your baby than feeding or changing him.

Registering the birth is good for you

The birth of a child has to be registered and there is a link between signing the birth certificate and how good a dad you'll be. Truly, truly! Kiernan (2006) compared fathers who had signed their baby's birth certificate with those who had attended the birth but not signed. Dads who signed the birth certificate scored higher on all measures of involvement. That was true even of fathers who were not, and still are not, living with the mother of their child.

I have argued that, when a woman tells a man she is carrying his child, it is one of those key moments in life. So is the birth. She who has just been through it deserves many rewards.

David Carr Brown's first wife was a Frenchwoman and a florist. That meant 'it was always very important to get the flowers right . . . otherwise I was in deep shit,' he told me. It depends on what you can afford. But try to afford something as I have yet to know the woman who didn't like to be offered flowers, chocolate or jewellery. I write at the start of 2009 when we are all broke so love may mean that all you can offer your loved one may be one rose, one half bar of healthy chocolate or a trinket you get for a fiver but it will still show you are thinking of her.

Cot deaths

Babies are vulnerable so never be afraid of going to the GP. If you have a baby or a young child, any surgery should make an appointment quickly available. If the surgery is too busy (which it should not be), Accident and Emergency departments will give babies priority. Never be ashamed of a few panics soon after the birth. Hormones, we now know, aren't just flooding through her but through you.

The statistics urge caution. Six babies die in every 1,000 live births in the UK. Rates in infant mortality in Britain are high by European standards and are usually linked to socio-economic status. New parents need to know about cot deaths which are a baffling exception in class terms. The latest view is that the baby should be put on her or his back on a flat surface. Do not put the baby face down. Do not smoke near the baby. Be careful about the mattress you have. And it may be a good idea to have a fan working in the baby's room.

Breast is best?

Dads need to understand what were once seen as women's mysteries. The World Health Organisation recommends exclusive breastfeeding for the first six months. A pamphlet produced by the National Childbirth Trust reassures that:

- The more the baby feeds, the more milk the mother makes.
- Babies are usually less windy, and put on weight better, if they finish feeding from the first breast before being offered the second so that they get plenty of the fat-rich milk.

- The baby needs to open his mouth really wide and have his chin against his mother's breast to feed well, as he massages the milk out with his tongue.
- Nipple soreness or pain during feeding is generally a sign that the baby is not getting a good mouthful of breast.

Men may find that women get very angry if they trot out this well meaning advice. One mother described to me that experience of breastfeeding as having a 'cheese grater on your tits'. She had little patience with men, midwives or doctors who told her to persevere.

The National Childbirth Trust (NCT) tries to reassure men. They shouldn't be uncomfortable if the mother wants to breastfeed in public. 'In reality, there is usually little or no breast showing when the baby is feeding.'

The pamphlet even gives fathers advice on how to keep mother motivated if she wants to give up because her nipples are cracked or she thinks her milk is not flowing right. Fathers should check that their baby is 'well latched'.

Previously I thought it was just doors that were latched! Then comes a question even Freud did not ask.

'Will breastfeeding affect our sex life?'

Tiredness may affect it more, the NCT suggests. Dropping any pretence of romance, the pamphlet says you may have to plan love making. Again the NCT offers advice to men that once would have been considered the kind of stuff men didn't need to know:

A woman's vagina may be drier during breastfeeding so using a lubricating gel can help.

Any breast stimulation can cause milk to flow so keep a soft towel handy; this is less of a problem if the mother feeds the baby before making love.

You may even find that your partner is more comfortable with her body as a result of giving birth and breast-feeding and enjoys sex more.

I wonder if men who dare offer advice on how to breastfeed might not be bonkers and risk injury but the NCT has no doubts that dads can be breastfeeding gurus without making total tits of themselves. Here is the advice they say you should give to the mother:

- offer both breasts at a feed, if you are not already doing so; this increases the volume of milk taken at a feed;
- express any surplus milk and offer it to the baby after breast feeds, preferably using a cup or spoon rather than a bottle.

The pamphlet offers helpful suggestions if there are problems: 'Boost your partner's confidence by encouraging her, like any new skill, with reassurance and praise.'

Patronising? Never!

All this information men get shows how attitudes are changing. We are all meant to be less mysterious now!

One reason breastfeeding is popular is that the latest wisdom is that it provides the ideal feeding mix as long as the mother does not drink, smoke, take drugs and eats healthily herself consuming her daily five portions of fruit and veg.

My baby is too fat, too small, too thin, too big

You should not drive yourself mad over the weight of your baby. Doctors expect a baby to lose up to 10 per cent of his or her birth weight in the days after birth. So a baby who weighs 3.3 kilos at birth might lose 330 grams and check in at just over 2.9 kilos. Babies should put it back on within 10–14 days.

The National Childbirth Trust suggests it is best to work out how much weight a baby puts on from the lowest weight reached rather than become too obsessed with the weight at birth. Babies usually gain at least 450 g (1 lb) in a month during the first three months. The crunch is around two weeks after birth. If your baby has not gained weight by then, take him or her to your doctor.

Dr Freud – why did you not write about nappies?

Freud liked to think of himself as a pioneer but even he, I suspect, would not have imagined that a respected charity, the National Childbirth Trust, would one day produce a pamphlet called *What's in a Nappy* which faces up to the fact that parents worry about what comes out, as well as about what goes in.

It's official now. A thriving baby will produce at least six really wet nappies a day after the first week and two substantial poohs a day. The pamphlet is colourful and says that 'the pooh is black and tarry (called meconium) after birth, but then changes during the first few days and by day 5 or 6 is yellow and runny'. One of my editors describes it as 'like chicken korma, can have greenish flecks like parsley'. Some breastfed babies may only produce one very large pooh every few days, or even less often. A baby who has dryish nappies and scanty poohs is not taking in enough milk.

It is best to err on the side of caution. Do not feel embarrassed about rushing to your doctor or summoning the health visitor to get the professional view on your baby's pooh. Yes, you have to take the nappy along and unroll it before the GP. Aileen and I did it. Good GPs will peer and pronounce just what the nappy means.

Helping means being vigilant

Babies are individual, no two are the same. What is normal and healthy is not set in stone. Your baby may reach some developmental milestones faster than average and lag behind a bit on others. Nevertheless it's a good idea to be aware of some problems which could be serious. I have put in here a long-ish list because it is better to get help than to worry. Parents should talk to their doctor if they see their baby has:

- stiffness or tight muscles
- extreme floppiness
- spots in the eyes.

By the time the baby is 12 to 15 weeks, worrying signs that a doctor should be consulted over include:

- if the baby is only using one side of the body or favouring a particular arm or leg
- if the baby does not seem to get better at controlling the movements of his or her head
- if the baby doesn't react to loud noises or bright lights
- if the baby shows no interest in reaching for objects or putting objects in his or her mouth
- if the baby never tries to roll over or sit up.

If by the age of five months the baby does not:

- fix his or her gaze at objects.

In all these instances it is better to get advice sooner rather than later.

Most babies will develop normally but at their own pace – and sometimes surprise you when they do something you really didn't expect like Nicholas did when he was six months old and we laughed and laughed at each other. Recently I met a toddler who at the age of two and a half gave a lovely description of how strange it was to go up in the London Eye and be way above the city. Freud said he was astonished by how fast 'the little primitive' became part of society. The old analyst was spot on. If he'd met Charlie, he'd have smiled at a toddler who wouldn't be remotely primitive very soon.

6

Love at first cry

In the last six months I've been visited by one baby and one two-year-old. Both were just with their mothers. Both women had had troubles in their lives – histories of drug abuse in the case of Katy and a string of pretty useless men in the case of Jenny. Katy is in her mid-twenties, Jenny ten years older. In dealing with their small children, these women were brilliant. They cooed, hugged, talked to their small children. I don't suppose for a moment that either of them had ever read the work of John Bowlby but he would have approved of them.

I interviewed John Bowlby in the 1970s and he seemed a very severe man to me. The fact that he had a bowler hat was enough for me to put him down as a bit of a stiff. I was there, however, not to analyse his hats but his theory: 'attachment theory', one of the key ideas in research on parenting since the Second World War.

Bowlby's breakthrough study looked at 44 juvenile thieves (Bowlby, 1981). Many of them had been separated from their mothers early in their lives. Bowlby was something of a Freudian and argued there is a complex interplay between the loving mother and baby who needs love. If she does not bond with her child, the baby starts life 'feeling' insecure. It's a dance in which the mother has to smile at, hold and love the child. A child needs a secure 'attached' base from which to grow, learn and explore the world. No secure base makes for insecurity and insecurity leads to failure. But some mothers do not bond instantly or feel an immediate overwhelming flood of love and many feel guilty about it.

When Bowlby practised, few thought the father was crucial. In a 400 page book on attachment, Bowlby devotes about four pages to fathers. When Aileen and I had our first son, Nicholas Joshua, we read what was then seen as the Bible, Dr Spock's *Baby and Child Care*; it was already in its thirteenth edition. Spock was also Freudian but dad only deserved about 10 pages out of 500.

Children did need fathers – thanks O Spocko, nearly as logical as your namesake on *Star Trek* – but there was no point the mother forcing pa to spend too much time with the little ones. She'd be wise to wait till junior was more like a real person before inflicting him, or her, on dad. Dad should try to spend an hour in 'rough-housing' play with the kids. But if work and the commute had left him too zonked to romp, dad shouldn't feel guilty but eat his dinner and relax in front of television. Bowlby was possibly even more mother-centric than Dr Spock.

But psychologists have slowly realised what we've known since Adam and Eve – a child needs both parents. There is maybe now more research than ever before into fathering (Lamb and Tamis-Lemonda, 2004) but such work faces a practical problem. Babies don't talk and can't be interviewed so they can't tell us what they feel or think. So psychologists have had to devise non-verbal methods to discover what infants think and feel.

The best known is the Strange Situation Procedure, devised in the 1960s, by Mary Ainsworth. Her idea was to see how infants who have different histories of bonding behave. Researchers watch a child playing for 20 minutes; his mother, father and strangers come and go and there are eight different 'conditions'. Sometimes mother leaves and the child is left alone or with a stranger. Then, the mother or father comes back. Sometimes the stranger talks to the parent so the child does not get undivided attention.

What interests psychologists is how much the child 'explores'. Does she or he play with new toys or just do nothing? What happens as mum, dad, stranger walk in and out? The results are pretty consistent. A child who is securely attached to its mother explores freely and will engage with the strangers. When mother goes away, the child will be upset; when the mother comes back, he or she will be happy to see her and go to her. Children, Bowlby argued, can explore best – and with zest – when they know they have a secure base to return to.

Not all parents can give such security. Some mothers and fathers – and one must remember that many of them will have been brought up by less than perfect parents who, in turn, were brought up by less than perfect parents – can only give 'anxious-ambivalent insecure attachment'. If parents can't, or don't, offer consistent affection and attention, the baby becomes anxious and unsure. Put in A Strange Situation, such a baby does not explore and does not interact with a stranger, even when the mother is there. When she leaves the room, the poor mite is crippled by anxiety, freezes or panics. When she comes back, the infant will try to stay close to her but, then suddenly, irrationally, may hit or push her. At this point, the baby with insight gets on the phone to make a first appointment with a therapist and babbles, 'My parents are inadequate. Help.' Anxiety-ambivalence is not the most potentially damaging of parenting styles, however.

Some parents are so inconsistent, their babies only get 'anxious-avoidant insecure attachment'. The anxious-avoidant infant ignores his mother, shows little emotion when she leaves, and just as little when she returns. The child may even run away if his parent tries to pick him up. Such an infant will not explore much even if his mother or father are present.

About 60–65 per cent of children seem to be 'securely attached' to their mothers, but not everyone thinks A Strange Situation is flawless. Professor Sir Michael Rutter, one of the world's leading child psychiatrists, argues the test 'is by no means free of limitations as it is very dependent on brief separations and reunions having the same meaning for all children'. Rutter draws attention to different cultures such as Japan (Miyake *et al.*, 1985) 'where infants are rarely separated from their mothers in ordinary circumstances'. He concludes sensibly that 'despite its manifest strengths, the procedure is based on just 20 minutes of behaviour. It can be scarcely expected to tap all the relevant qualities of a child's attachment relationships.'

Children who are securely attached to their mothers usually thrive. They develop well physically, intellectually and socially. There is less work on fathers but enough to hint at problems if fathers do not bond.

Norwegian men get six weeks paid leave of absence from work when they become a father. Since 1993 the number who take all six weeks has risen from only 4 per cent to 85 per cent so they have more time to bond. Many Norwegian men have discovered the joys of spending time with their children. You can see them with their children in city parks, or taking them to a football game. Some fathers even cook with their children. But the study by Storo and Jansen (2006) warns against complacency. When they go back to work, many Norwegian men still find it hard to insist on leaving on time to spend quality time with their kids. It has not even helped that two Norwegian leaders are competing for the Top Dad of the Arctic Prize. (They'd have no hope in the Antarctic where penguins win, as Masson argued.) Crown Prince Haakon Magnus and the Prime Minister Jens Stoltenberg have said they have to give priority to their own children. Running the country comes second. Change the nappies first! Despite these role models, many Norwegian men still feel it is not very manly to look after children.

Yet good fathering makes a big difference. Secure father–child attachment is associated with fewer behaviour problems when the child is older (Verschueren and Marcoen, 1999). A child who has bonded with his father tends to be more sociable and to interact better with other children (Parke, 2002).

Causes for concern

Bonding means paying attention both for fun and to spot worrying warning signs. New dads should worry if they do not see signs of the following:

If by the time the baby is roughly nine months, he or she is not trying ever to sit up.

If by the time the baby is roughly 15 months old, he or she is making no attempt to pull themselves up to make first attempts to walk.

If by the time the baby is 24 months, he or she is not making sounds which may not yet be words but are pre-words.

Trust versus mistrust

The psychoanalyst Erik Erikson looked at the choices children make, and have made for them, at crucial points in their lives. The first 'choice' is trust versus mistrust, he said. If a baby cries and is picked up and comforted, he or she will learn to trust. If the baby is left to cry when she's hungry or dirty, she will learn to distrust because the lesson of her life has been that no one listens or cares or does anything when she or he cries. Everything you can do to create trust will last them for the rest of their lives.

The more you cuddle, hold and look at your baby the more you will bond. Men do hold their kids more than they used to. Harvey (1980) found that 32 per cent of men held their babies in the hour after delivery. In the early 1980s that rose to half but some research suggests that men are still often timid about touching their babies. Usually, they first touch the baby on the feet and toes. Fathers are unlikely to smother love their children to death, as John B. Watson feared. Praise is due to a tribe of Nigerian pygmies called the Akas; they spend 20 per cent of their time holding their children, more than any other group of men on earth. They should be our inspiration.

Self Analysis 4
Ask yourself:
Do you feel diffident about touching your baby?
Are you scared of hurting the baby?
Are you scared that your feelings will overwhelm you?
Does touching your child seem somehow wrong or disgusting?
Is this the way you feel about small animals?
Can you begin to imagine what might alter your feelings?

Being anxious is nothing to be ashamed of. First-time fathers have usually not had much practice holding babies and babies are so small, so fragile. Their skulls still have that terrifying gap where the fontanelles have not yet become solid.

I was lucky. I was never frightened of holding my babies though I was very terrified of how fragile they were. And I hate cuddling cats, dogs, kittens. But I learned, and any man can learn. Relax before you pick up the baby. Smile at the baby. Enjoy touching your child.

Our anxieties about child abuse have made the question of what is appropriate touching fraught. But it is really a matter of common sense. Do not play with the baby's genitals but stroke its head, its arms, its feet. Touching is the best way of developing your bond with your baby. Many men find that stroking their child calms them down and it is a good way of dealing with stress. Dr Spock was wrong. If Executive Man had come home and cuddled his children, he would have been happier as he felt the tensions of his day ebb. Then he could have settled down to his evening cocktail with a soppy smile on his face still dandling his kids on his knee.

Sweet! And very effective psychologically!

7

Tensions for parents

Having a small child is one of the most stressful events we live through. There is evidence of that from research using the Life Events scale. The fact that it is a happy event does not mean there is no stress. It is also getting worse because as Janice Turner noted in the London *Times* (18 October 2008) 'parental obligation has mushroomed'. She recalled spending time with her first child in smart West London playgrounds and making fun of American parents. 'While we Brits slumped hung over on benches with coffee and Sunday papers, US mothers were getting down and dirty in the sandpit.' Kids had to be monitored and rewarded. Every time Yankee kid made a mud pie, mum (who had read every do-it-yourself parenting book since El Spocko) would yell 'Good job.' It didn't matter if the mud pie was shaped all wrong.

Turner described the sand pit wars. 'If two tots disputed ownership of a bucket, these moms piled in like a UN Peacekeeping detail.'

Some years later – i.e. now – Turner can't mock because British middle class chattering class parents have gone the American way. She blames Madonna and Gwyneth Paltrow who 'began breeding in London, transfixing us with their glamorous maternity wardrobes, fast returning figures and macrobiotic packed lunches'.

Turner's lament that mothers feel under intense pressure will not make it easy for dads.

I managed to be not that useful in the weeks after both Nicholas and Reuben were born. My excuse was that as I worked for myself I had to work or we'd starve!

I remember endlessly ringing Aileen to explain why I was coming home late. The trains were late; the traffic was terrible; I had to rush and do an interview on which the fate of the world depended. I thought my ringing showed that I hadn't forgotten her. She thought 'crap' and that I was ringing her to make myself feel better. In those days I didn't have a mobile phone, that great instrument which makes constant dysfunctional couple communication possible. Someone should write a PhD on mobile phones and marital dissatisfaction.

With mothers stuck at home and fathers working, problems start and can get serious. A study in 1986 found that in the year after a child was born, the 'level of marital satisfaction' changed in 40 per cent of relationships (Belsky and Pensky, 1988). The study compared how couples saw the relationship at three points – when they knew a baby was on the way, when the baby was born and when their child was one year old. Some couples were so happy to be parents nothing else mattered. But 25 per cent felt somewhat less satisfied; for 10 per cent, having a baby triggered serious dissatisfaction.

The reasons were often complex. The parents got tired, the men felt they were being neglected, the mother was more in love with the baby than with them. The mothers felt their lives had narrowed. One woman referred to life with baby as 'the home prison'.

There is the question of sex too. In Tennessee Williams' great play *Cat on a Hot Tin Roof*, Big Daddy observes that most problems in most marriages start in bed. The man wants the woman who doesn't want him or the woman wants the man who doesn't want her. New babies affect sex lives very often.

Sex when the nipper's next door

Rosalind Miles almost seems to approve of mothers who lose interest in sex. The man's done his job. Can't expect more of the sperm producer. Concentrate on the children. Just before the split of the decade, *The News of the World* revealed Guy Ritchie and Madonna did not have sex for 18 months while Madonna adopted children and focused on her concerts and childcare. Since Miles is interested in psychotherapy, I can't help fantasising about one of these 'no sex please I'm a mother now' mothers explaining to her kids ten years later: 'Oh I stopped having a sex life, kiddo, when you were born. I was really glad . . . It was what I really wanted all along . . . a chance to be frigid . . . and frustrate your dad.' We all know how the Madonna and Guy saga ended.

The National Childbirth Trust survey went back to its sample of 817 fathers six months after their children were born. Only 53 per cent answered and these were probably the men who were most involved with children. Most men said the birth had been a wonderful experience and that they loved helping with the childcare. It brought out their feminine side. But 33 per cent of these men also reported a decline in their sex life; the larger 2000 survey found over 50 per cent of men said they had less sex, usually because of tiredness.

For many women 'what used to be their sex life can now become his appetite alone,' Miles argues. If your partner has just snatched five hours sleep and is dreading the baby starting to cry at 2 a.m, she is hardly likely to 'welcome her husband's advances with yelps of joy and open arms and legs'. Some 40 per cent of women did not welcome sex three months after childbirth because of pain during intercourse according to a recent study at the University of Minnesota.

Miles pokes fun at one man who was finally driven to beg 'but I only want ten minutes of your time'. Miles is right in saying men have no right to expect sex from their wives or partners. You have to be Mr Hardon Crass to get truly fed up if your wife or partner does not want to make love three or four months after she has given birth. But, what if it doesn't change? After six months, maybe it's reasonable to worry and, at least, to want to talk about no love making. After nine months it certainly is so, but Miles seems to suggest that if a man wants to do that it's oppressive.

The French say one person kisses, the other one permits the kiss. One person wants: the other is wanted. It always needs courage to raise questions of desire, of why you are no longer making love. You can never be sure what your lover will say. It may be that she has stopped fancying you; it may be he has a lover. It's bound to be difficult, but if you don't discuss it, what will happen to the relationship? People do not put up with cold 1930s marriages easily these days.

Self Analysis 5
Ask yourself:

If you have had children has it damaged your sex life?
What stops you talking about it with your wife/partner?
Do you feel less desire?
Does she feel less desire? Or are you too tired, or too ratty to go there?

It's not easy to preserve your relationship while taking good care of your new baby. I suggest a few basics. I know these are counsels of perfection and that perfection is never harder to attain than when you feel unloved and are unlaid. But try.

Make the space, time and bubble in which you can be together as a couple again. Try having sex at different times – not just before going to sleep but maybe after you have managed to settle the baby or, if she's napping, before dinner.

Use imagination. You can't just nip out to have an Indian, talk it through and come back to bed as you used to do. So make a special meal and take nothing for granted.

Listen more than you complain.

Try not to get angry or resentful.

Try to understand how she feels.

Try to agree things you can do which will take some of the bitterness out of the situation.

As Miles herself suggests, the reasons a woman may not want to make love may be more complex and very private. You need to coax them out.

One curiosity – having a son seems to disrupt a marriage more than having a girl but, paradoxically, for men a son seems to make it harder to leave the marriage. They may be less happy but they don't leave; many say they have an obligation to their son.

Source: www.CartoonStock.com

I'd rather stick my head up a dragon than have sex

Until they had a baby George and Jeanette used to make love many mornings but that changed because they were so tired. One of them often had to get up at 3 a.m. to feed the baby. The baby was crying and had to be changed all the time. You can't have sex if you're dead and Jeanette felt dead or, at least, more tired than she had ever done in her life. George was frustrated and Jeanette was furious. She was furious because he made it clear he was frustrated. He was furious because he was frustrated. She was also anxious because of their history. George was not the faithful type. He expected his nookie once a week. Jeanette began to worry that he might be flirting or sleeping with someone at the office, she told me.

Jeanette became so angry at herself for worrying about it that their sex life stopped totally. They would sleep, not touching, in the same bed. When he tried to touch her, she rebuffed him. She liked that because she had power over him. But it took her years to admit that not lovely trait to herself, she told me.

Sometimes, birth affects men in a bizarre way. Jack McHarris teaches at one of the local universities on Merseyside. He was pleased to be a father again but surprised that it seemed to destroy his sex drive or, at least, his physical desire for his wife. 'I just did not find her desirable at all. I mean I've no idea if she'd gone off me as well because I really just stopped fancying her.'

Two years on, McHarris and his wife have separated. She now lives in the Yorkshire moors while he has returned to Aberdeen. He still feels guilty and a little perplexed about the way he lost all his lust and why, when he still found her beautiful, his wife aroused absolutely no desire.

Both these couples were unable to talk honestly to each other. But sex is not the only source of friction – pun intended – in the weeks and months after a baby is born.

Snore your way to happiness – probably not

Nicholas was four months old. Aileen felt she had no time and energy to write. She had started an MPhil but she was about to give up on the idea. When I got home one evening Aileen handed me our son as if he were a thing. She was half in tears and livid. Nicholas had been crying and crying for hours; she had been trying to comfort him but he just kept bawling. She had to sleep. She just couldn't take it any more.

I wasn't exactly full of beans myself. I was making *Anatomy of a Pin Up*, a short film about the Penthouse Organisation. The producer, Walter Shenson, had produced the Beatles' films. If he liked my work, all kinds of doors might open but Shenson was a tough boss. I also had to cope with his neurotic assistant, a cameraman who didn't understand why he was working for a director who was 20 years younger than he was, the bizarre politics of the Penthouse Organisation, not to mention girlie models. Many of them had an unusual problem Freud had never worried about.

How would the fathers of the models feel when they saw them nude in Penthouse?

Psychologists should study that one.

I was in no mood to take our son who was crying. Aileen went to sleep. I expected her to be grateful which, of course, she wasn't, especially as I had to go off the next morning on location. I don't claim to remember the dialogue as they do in misery memoirs but it wouldn't have been too different from:

Her: 'So you're off again.'
Him: 'I've got to go work.'
Her: 'You don't care I'm an effing prisoner.'
Him: 'I love you.'

'Fuck off' Aileen added, with a parting shot that I was sure to be late again.

Aileen's mother was so worried by the tone of her letters she flew in on a rescue mission from America to help us cope.

I was not the most loving, attentive or sensitive husband then and I am ashamed of that. It was only when the children were much older that I was able to hear how isolated and cut-off Aileen felt at the time, and how my behaviour did not help. We both paid for it. Would talking better have solved it all? Probably not everything, but it would have dealt with some of it.

I list a series of typical rows that parents of young children have.

Rows about time – you can go out; I am stuck in the home prison.
Rows about housework – you never do anything, idle sod.
Rows about shopping.
Rows about money – you waste our money down the pub.
Rows about doing your share of the care – you never get up at night to give him the bottle.
Rows about ignoring the other person – I might as well not be here.
Rows about your parents – you think your mum knows more about the baby than I do.

Rows about the relationship in general – we don't talk any more.

Rows about sex – you don't fancy me any more.

More rows about sex – we don't make love any more or making love has become very boring.

Rows about the other children and how they respond to the baby.

Rows about who is more tired.

Rows about who is the greater victim. Is it better to be the one at work or the one looking after the baby?

Every couple will have its own flashpoints.

Try to identify what these are – and, then, I keep coming back to the value of humour. Couples who can laugh at themselves can, at least, not get totally sucked into their rows. I have therefore developed the Hold Horns High routine into a real therapeutic instrument.

Mustn't grumble game

Sit opposite each other. Get into the Hold Horns High position with your arms up above your head. Then put your right arm on your left shoulder and your left arm on your right shoulder and say 'Mustn't grumble'.

You then say 'Mustn't grumble . . . but'.

Then you each say just what it is you have to grumble about.

The other person then cross examines;

'Is that all you have to grumble about?'

Couples who are desperately unhappy will not manage to hold horns high – it does need a basic mateyness – but couples who are fed up, but want to make it better, will probably be able to play it. I have yet to do the definitive experiment but I know that a good and regular grumbling keeps a relationship happy and healthy – like good and regular sex. I can not prove the grumble part scientifically yet, but many of the worst problems I have had in relationships were due to the fact that we did not grumble in time about things before they became disastrous.

Dealing with problems as they happen is vital, as research on mediation in divorce shows that couples get so angry and disappointed that they blame each other for everything that has gone wrong. It sounds preachy but the only way through is to talk, say how you feel, listen to how the other person feels, compromise and change. There is no hard evidence to suggest that men are worse at doing this than women, according to American researcher, Deborah Tannen, probably the world's leading expert on how women and men row – and what language they use (Tannen, 1991).

You need, in the midst of all this flak, to remember your one common interest.

Your little bundle of joy who won't go to sleep, has sicked up over your shirt and is driving you mad. But love is often maddening. Grown ups should be resigned to that.

8

The newborn baby is no fool

Once, the newborn baby was seen as a chaotic confusion of reflexes and brain cells firing, with 'synaptic exuberance'. Someone somewhere will have done a video installation to music called *Brain – Exuberance*. The music should be the allegro from Bach's Brandenburg Concerto No. 1 which goes quicker and quicker and quicker, the notes firing off each other just like neurons.

If no one's done it, it's my idea.

Newborn babies are supposed to be just a bundle of reflexes so I'd like to start by highlighting that they have one remarkable skill – they can imitate some actions of adults.

Play dreams and imitation

Imitation is not a simple business. Infantile imitation needs to be analysed. To imitate what I have just done: first, you have to notice I am there, then, you have to register what I have done, third, you have to have the conscious ability to reproduce or parody my actions.

The Swiss child psychologist, Jean Piaget (1896–1980) offered telling examples in *Play, Dreams and Imitation in Childhood* (1952). The first imitations were vocal. One of his children T. at 2 months 11 days said 'la' and 'le'. 'I reproduced them. He repeated them seven times out of nine slowly and distinctly' (p. 9). These first imitations might be just reflexes, but by the age of four to five months, Piaget was sure babies were showing signs of intelligence. At five months, one of his daughters, J. was imitating him quite clearly because when he stuck his tongue out at her, she stuck her tongue back out at him.

In the 1980s, the evidence became dramatically stronger. Meltzoff and Moore (1983) found babies could imitate an adult opening his mouth and sticking out his tongue almost as soon as they were born. They saw a 30-minute-old baby do just that. (Does it say something about human beings that our first act is sticking our tongue out at other human beings?) One of the best studies was done in Nepal. Reissland (1988) found newborn Nepalese babies could imitate an adult sticking out the tongue, or pursing his lips, or widening his lips.

This 'skill', psychologists found, lasted usually till the baby was 21 days. Then it disappeared as suddenly as it had appeared; then it reappeared when the infant was about six months old. Piaget's daughter stuck her tongue out at her eminent dad when she was five months old, we have seen. The important question is: why are babies born with this ability to imitate? Is it endearing behaviour that will motivate adults to bond with and protect them? The baby rewards the adult by providing something 'cute' to respond to. Stroke me and I'll smile. I'll even poke my tongue out to make you sit up and notice.

It is not just babies who imitate. Macaque monkeys, scientists have been amazed to learn, have a 'mirroring' neuron which allows baby monkeys to reproduce some actions they have just seen. Recent evidence shows that normal babies have such mirroring neurons.

The behaviourist John B. Watson is probably kicking himself for not seeing that back in 1914 when he studied babies in Baltimore, Ohio, but he was also quite impressed with newborns. Thirty minutes after being born babies could turn their heads. A 14-hour-old baby could co-ordinate his movements to stare at a light right in front of him; three hours later, the baby could turn his head and stare at a light that was 20 degrees to his right or left.

Watson's research could be simple but also amusing. Watson even claimed babies can swim or, at least, make reflex swimming movements which keep them afloat. Once he pinched the baby's nose and waited to see what the baby did. One angry baby's hand went up at once and pushed at the experimenter's fingers. Impressive muscular co-ordinations, Watson deduced. He also observed smiles, most powerful of social signals a baby can send. He saw one instance of a four-day-old baby smiling. Other babies smiled on the seventh or eighth day, usually when stroked gently or tickled lightly.

Myrtle McGraw, a famous Canadian paediatrician, argued that after birth the baby's reflexes are better organised than scientists believe. Babies can grasp automatically, for example. McGraw found reflexes then become more chaotic and disorganised. This seemed weird, suggesting the baby was suddenly even more helpless than at birth. But the biology has its logic. Very fixed instincts would make it harder for babies to develop; they need a flexible nervous system to get on with the important business of making new connexions, of learning and co-ordination.

The social awareness of the newborn, Freud's little primitive, is not that primitive. John Morton and colleagues at the Medical Research Council's Cognitive Development Unit showed in 2000 that babies recognise their mothers' faces from four days after birth. How no one knows. Logically the mirroring neurons would not explain it.

By five weeks, the baby does not even have to see the whole face to recognise its mother. Morton and his team blacked out the shape of the mother's head and her hair. All the babies had to go on were the face's inner features (i.e. the set of the mouth, the eyes, the nose) but that was enough for most of them to recognise their mum (Bartrip *et al.*, 2001).

How fast does the baby's brain work?

Some recent research has tried to work out how quickly babies process information. The experiments had to be inventive. Babies were trained to respond to triangles or squares. Perhaps surprisingly the newborn seems to process information as fast as toddlers do as the reaction times of very young babies and one- and two-year-olds are the same

(Salthouse, 1998). But speed is not everything. Young babies cannot concentrate, so they often fail when given something complex to do.

Don't immediately start reading philosophy to your three-month-old, but do provide lots of games, contact and stimulation from the very start.

Silly faces

These findings suggest a nice game and, again, humour helps. Stick your tongue out, widen your lips, make utterly silly faces – and see if you can get your baby to make himself look as stupid as you. (We'll assume that the babies aren't being ironic!)

Many fathers do the following automatically, but here are some simple things you can do with your baby which will help bond and also be good fun.

1 Look at your child and smile.
2 Tickle his or her feet. Babies laugh when they are tickled from two to three months, but they can't tickle themselves so you need to take part.
3 Put your fingers out so the baby can grasp them which tests the grasp reflex. A grasping baby is a good thing.
4 Stroke the baby gently.
5 Make absurd noises. As I aim to provide multi-media advice I will be offering my own CD of absurd noises.
6 Hold the baby safely up above your head.
7 Play peek-a-boo, a game which teaches a great many social skills. By the time they are 12 months old, some babies can initiate the game.
8 Watch for the baby imitating you. Do not get impatient or scared if the baby cries. Babies do cry. It is their way of making contact. If your baby never cries, then is the time to worry.

Remember in all these games to let your baby set the pace. This is not an exam. When your baby turns away, closes his or her eyes, or gets fussy, take a break. Babies need time and space. Adapting to your baby's needs will help build your baby's trust in you.

You will remember your baby's first steps, your baby's first words, your baby's first sentence – vividly. They are sweet and precious. But your child won't have the slightest recollection of them. So I return to my advice: dads should keep a diary, and even a video diary, because little Billy will never be a week old again.

I am very aware of this as I write today. One of my relatives has just died in Israel. Her daughter has sent me six photographs of her mother. In one of them my grandmother and my mother are looking at a baby. It's me. In the chaos of my teens, this photo got lost or mislaid. I've never had a picture of myself so little before. It makes me smile – and weep. I'm much pudgier now.

Keep that diary.

Source: www.CartoonStock.com

9

How the baby's mind develops and the eternal puzzle – nature or nurture?

In *The Third Man*, the great film about Vienna after the war, Harry Lime, played by Orson Welles, gives his innocent friend a lecture on life and Switzerland. Centuries of peace have not made the Swiss very creative. Their greatest achievements have been the cuckoo clock and good chocolate. Harry Lime was wrong because some of the most important ideas about child psychology came from Geneva.

The child psychologist Jean Piaget published his first scientific paper when he was 11. He was living about 40 miles from Geneva in Neuchatel. Piaget was immensely clever and started when he was 20 to work on how children develop. It took him about 15 years to arrive at a theory of four stages of development which dominated child psychology from 1926 on.

Many of Piaget's ideas came from observing his own children meticulously. The Piaget children, Jacqueline (born 1925), Lucienne (born 1927) and Laurent (born 1931), were studied from the moment they were born. Child development theory is still very much based on how these three Swiss children grew up in a very different culture 80 years ago.

Piaget argued that children's minds develop in four main stages:

1 the sensory-motor stage
2 the preoperational stage
3 the stage of concrete operations
4 the stage of formal operations.

Piaget was brought up at a time when children were taught formal logic. Formal operations were logical operations. He had what seems to us the weird idea that most teenagers are logically competent and can see the flaws in complex arguments. Piaget's teens would never have watched *Big Brother* or read celeb mags. More of that later.

Children's minds develop in an intricate but natural pattern, Piaget argued. There was not a 'normal' age for a child to go into any of his stages and he loathed the American mania, as he put it, for pushing children. Inevitably, though, psychologists have tended to put average ages against the stages.

A little primitive – Sigmund Freud

Political correctness was not an issue in the 1920s in Geneva and Piaget likened babies not just to savages but to primitive savages! William James, one of the first men to set up a psychology lab back in 1879, wrote that babies were a blooming buzzing confusion. Freud – and he had six of them – called the baby 'a little primitive' as we have seen.

The newborn is unaware of the most basic fact of life. When I touch someone I know where I end and they begin – what is my skin and what is their skin. Piaget argued that babies must learn this crucial distinction. The newborn does not realise he is a separate being and that his body – and his self – stops at the ends of his fingers and the ends of his toes. Beyond that, the world is other people, other things. The infant 'looks at his own body the way we look at a strange animal', because 'the baby is submerged in a chaos of interesting impressions without there being any distinction between his internal state and things outside' (Piaget, 1952).

For a father, a baby is both strange and an adorable extension of himself. This is a feeling you need to guard against from the very beginning. Your baby is not a second you, not a replica, but a unique human being with whom you do have a unique relationship. One of the joys of parenthood is seeing the key steps as the baby grows – the first smile, the first step, the first pull up on the cot.

Self Analysis 6
Try to imagine the questions a baby might ask if a baby could talk. This baby is quite intellectual.
What am I?
What are those things that move above my cot?
Are they living?
What is out there that is like me?
Where does out there start and in here end?
Can I affect it?
But the first step to becoming a human being is more subtle.

Do you remember being a baby?

If you think you remember the first time you did something you meant to, you are probably deluding yourself. Most of us remember nothing of our baby lives and the first memories for most of us come from when we were three or four. So the moment you first saw a toy and said to yourself I want that, almost certainly you have forgotten.

Freud asked an interesting question: why do adults remember so little of their lives as babies or small children?

'Childhood amnesia', as Freud called it, is the result of the psycho-sexual conflicts the child faces – the Oedipus complex in boys and the Electra complex in girls. Young girls are also jealous, hate their mother and want their father's undivided attention. By the time boys and girls are three or four, they have learned the rules enough to 'know' these desires are forbidden as well as being unrealistic. So children repress these 'bad' desires but the repression devours so much psychic energy that all memories of early childhood are wiped out, repressed and suppressed.

Freud's ideas remain controversial a century after he first published them and there could be other more biological explanations for childhood amnesia. Maybe early memory traces are so unstable they literally break up or decompose in the brain; maybe they are buried so deep they cannot be accessed.

The question of when the baby intends to do something and does it, is key. Then, that baby is no longer a mewling chaos of reflexes but on the way to becoming a human being. It's a mark of being human that we intend our actions. Imagine the scene in court. Tom has murdered his wife but his barrister argues Tom didn't know what he was doing because he was mentally ill and incapable of forming an intention. If the jury believes that, they won't find him guilty.

The question is when can a baby first have an intention? When is an action not a reflex? Piaget saw the very first signs of these 'intentional' actions from 14 days on. He noticed the following.

When Jacqueline was two weeks old, Piaget saw that if he put his finger against her cheek, she turned her head and opened her little mouth as if to take the nipple.

At 23 days, Laurent searched for the nipple with his mouth. He would turn to the right to look for it if it brushed against him. None of that was meant or intentional, Piaget argued, but it was the first step in that direction.

By three months of age, Piaget's babies were more co-ordinated. If they heard a noise, they turned their heads to see what might be making it. They stared at objects and reached out for them. Human intelligence starts with these motor movements, especially with eye–hand co-ordination. Fathers should spend time with their babies giving them objects to touch, teasing them gently by showing them balls and toys and then taking them back. Doing that isn't just a nice game, it is also a way of helping babies discover an important lesson about physical reality.

Is the car park still there?

Piaget was not the first person to offer a strange theory about seeing objects. Bishop Berkeley, the seventeenth-century Irish philosopher, claimed 'esse est percipi', to be is to be perceived. When no one looks at a tree it isn't there, but the universe wasn't in constant flux because Berkeley, being a Bishop, said God was alert all the time and perceiving everything – including the fridge.

Babies do not have the concept of objects adults do, Piaget claimed. When I walk out of my front door, I don't worry whether the petrol station opposite my house still exists when I'm not looking at it. It could have burned down while I wasn't looking but, unless there is evidence of a dramatic change, I assume it will still be selling petrol. For adults objects are permanent. We start to worry if we think an object is there one minute and disappears the next. We need our daily assumptions. But babies don't have the experience to make these assumptions. They are at the mercy of 'the here and now'. If they don't see something, it just does not exist. It is beyond their ken, out of their universe.

Piaget then spotted something bizarre in the way six-month-old babies behaved.

In one of his most famous experiments, Piaget hid objects. Sometimes, he let the baby see where he was concealing them; sometimes, he did not. Remarkably this did not change matters much. Once the toy or ball disappeared, the baby under six months behaved as if said object had never existed. Piaget only had to throw a cloth over a toy, even while the baby was looking, for that to happen. The infant made no attempt to remove the cloth. Instead Piaget noted (1950, p. 132) 'the child acts as if the object were reabsorbed into the cloth'.

By ten months, the baby behaved even more peculiarly. When Piaget rolled a ball behind some cushions, a normal ten-month-old usually looked for the ball. But in the wrong place! A logical baby would look for the ball behind the cushions, but these 'older' babies started looking where the ball had been . . . before it disappeared. It was as if they believed the ball might reappear at that very spot by magic. It is a very curious result.

Piaget has been attacked for not looking systematically at alternative theories which might explain why babies failed at some tasks. We know now that babies follow objects with their eyes, even if they disappear. If a moving object goes behind a screen babies keep looking along the path where it should be moving. From the age of three months they are anticipating where it should be (Bower, 1989). Why do they do that, if the baby brain 'thinks' objects cease to exist the moment they don't see them?

Piaget's experiment is simple to do yourself in your home. Hide a furry animal or some other toy from your child while the child is looking. Then distract your child by making funny faces. Then see where she or he looks for it.

Many psychologists now believe that Piaget under-estimated quite badly what the infant knew or could work out. Fantz found, for instance, that newborns could differ-entiate red from green and that two-month-olds could discriminate all the basic colours. By the time they were three months most babies preferred yellow and red to blue and green. Newborns could also distinguish between their mother's face and a stranger's (unless both adults wore scarves), a four-month-old could recognise acquaintances, and a six-month-old had some sense of what feelings differ-ent facial expressions conveyed (Fantz, 1970).

'Core' systems

Fantz influenced many child psychologists. One is Elisabeth Spelke of Harvard University, who studies 'attentional persistence', the tendency of infants and children to gaze longer at something new, surprising, or different. Show a baby a toy elephant. By the third time the elephant appears, the baby will look at it for less long. Trunks are so yesterday. Give Jumbo four ears on its tenth appearance, and then watch. If the baby looks longer at the four eared elephant, it's reasonable to deduce the baby can see a difference between two and four. The technique makes the most of the one thing babies can control well: how long they look at an object (Spelke, 2007).

Spelke has also studied how babies recognise faces and objects and how they follow moving targets. Six-month-olds can distinguish 8 objects from 16, and 16 from 32, but not 8 from 12 or 16 from 24. The differences have to be great. When babies are shown someone reaching for one of two objects, 12-month-olds know which object the person will grab by looking at where he is looking. But the average eight-month-old does not 'know' enough to predict that well.

Spelke has developed a theory of 'core knowledge sys-tems'. She claims that we are born with basic cognitive skills and structures that let us make sense of objects, space, people, movement, and number. These cores form as our brains form in the womb, and they are specific. There is a core for colour, a core for movement and so on. Without these wired-in biological structures, everything would always remain William James' buzzing blooming confusion because these cores underpin all the skills and knowledge we later acquire – language, mathematics, even logic. Yet we almost completely ignore these foundations. We certainly can't find out about them by introspection.

The implications are profound and unexpected. Her findings, Spelke argues, show 'most of our cognitive workings are much like those of babies and are built on the core knowledge that we had as babies'.

So dads are really just like their little ones! Spelke sees this as grounds for hope, not pessimism. If all human beings are the same with 'intricate and rich system of core knowledge that everyone shares . . . that gives us common ground. In a world of so much conflict, I think that's something we badly need.'

One piece of evidence that supports Spelke's 'core' theory is musical.

Don't forget the music . . .

Peter Hepper at the University of Belfast asked mothers-to-be to listen to the signature tunes of television programmes such as *Neighbours*. After their babies were born, they responded more to that tune than to other music. This showed our memory systems begin to work, Hepper argued, while we are still in the womb. The foetus had to have stored the *Neighbours* tune, accessed it and retrieved it. It would be nice to imagine foetuses humming a tune or tapping their toes to a rhythm. Foetuses whose mothers do not smoke or drink remember tunes better! If there were not some musical 'core', Hepper's results would be hard to explain (Hepper, 1991).

The best evidence for memory in babies comes from studies by the American psychologist, Caroline Rovee Collier. She has been looking at infants as young as eight weeks. Babies cannot speak, so Rovee Collier too has had to be inventive.

If a toddler sees a toy, he or she can whoop 'there again'. The baby cannot say a word but the baby's movements will reflect that excitement. The rate at which babies kick when they are shown a mobile shows whether or not they remember, according to Rovee Collier. If babies remember nothing, it will not matter what particular mobile they are looking at and the researchers will know that because there will be no difference to the *kick rate* of the babies.

Remember the phrase '*kick rate*'. It offers the hope of understanding what the baby remembers.

Rovee Collier trains babies to kick when they see a mobile and establishes the average kick rate for each baby. Then, the babies get to see either a mobile decorated with the same stimuli the baby was 'trained on', or a new one. The kick rate 'tells' Rovee Collier whether the babies 'remember'. If a baby kicks more than their average, then that is 'yes, the same', but if a baby does not kick above the average, it's a 'no . . . this is any old mobile so I'll kick at my average rate'.

Some psychologists think her logic is not totally logical but Rovee Collier has got impressive, consistent results. Babies as young as eight weeks will kick far more at a mobile they have seen before than at a new mobile. Three-month-olds show near perfect memory for mobiles. The results also suggest infant memory seems to work much like adult memory works. Adults remember the first item of a set they are shown better than the rest. This is called the 'primacy effect'. Babies are just like adults in this; the mobile they saw first was remembered best. But the baby brain is limited.

In adults, it doesn't matter whether you show subjects 3 or 300 stimuli; the first stimulus will be still be more memorable. Babies can cope with three mobiles, but if you show them more than five mobiles they do not remember the first one better. The primacy effect vanishes. Baby memory no longer works like adult memory. The baby brain seems to suffer from the modern malaise of information overload.

Mobile memory

There is also the question of priming and, dads do not confuse your primacy with your priming. Think decorating. You have to prime before you put on the emulsion and, in psychology too, you have to prepare the surface. In one study, 30 three-month-olds were trained to kick to a mobile which had an S design on it. In effect, these infants were 'primed'. Two weeks later they were shown the S mobile again but this time the experimenter moved it about, instead of just dangling above their cots.

The next day, the babies' kick rate went well above the baseline level when a mobile with either the original S design, or a larger S, or a smaller S, was dangled above their cots. Rovee Collier argued this showed three-month-olds have two memory systems operating – one for stimuli the same size as the one first shown, and one where the size does not matter. This is very like adult memory systems.

Rovee Collier's work is controversial and some critics attack her for extrapolating too much. Does the rate of kicking truly relate to memory? Can you infer so much from mobiles? But she has many followers, like Kimberly Kraebel.

Kraebel studies subjects aged three and five months old. Her aim is to find out whether it helps babies to learn and remember if they are shown 'amodal' cues, cues that come from more than one of the senses. Kraebel uses a mobile made up of cylindrical shapes and a small motor that makes the mobile move. A ribbon connected to the mobile is looped around the baby's foot. When the baby kicks, the mobile moves; *Sesame Street* music is played for reinforcement.

While learning to make the mobile move, one group of babies holds a wooden cylinder, exactly the same shape as those on the mobile. The second group holds nothing; the third group holds a brick-shaped object. Again, the number of kicks the baby makes are recorded. Kraebel argues that the more a baby kicks, the more baby understands their kick moves the mobile.

Babies who hold the cylindrical object while learning to make a mobile of cylinders move kick more than two other groups – those who did not hold an object and those who hold the brick shape. Holding the brick actually inhibited learning. Babies do not learn better just because they are holding an object; the shape of that object must match the shape of what they are seeing. Only that helps with 'facilitated learning'. It's a strange finding but it seems that giving your baby plenty of experience with mobiles is a good, as well as a fun, thing (Kraebel, 2009).

In our house we always establish the kick rate: silly games

Be like your baby. Suspend the mobile from the ceiling, lie down as well by the side of the baby and kick when you see your baby kick. That way you can establish your own kick rate. And it'll be fun.

The next stage can become a family game. Best if mum and dad are there – and with a good watch. One of you lies down with the baby; the other one is the scientist.

Have two different mobiles – say a pink one and a striped one with no pink on it. Watch how much the baby kicks to each mobile during one minute. Say they kick 12 times to the pink and 8 to the striped, your baby's average 60-second kick score is 10. Watch how much the adult kicks to each mobile too.

Twenty-four hours later show the baby either one of these mobiles – and a brand new one. Establish the kick rate again. See if there is any difference between how much baby kicks to the old and the new mobile. If there is a difference, you have proved your baby is remembering.

The lessons for ambitious dads are clear. Put a small ball in your baby's hand – yes, dads, this is what you need to do if you want them to grow up to keep goal for Manchester United – and let them watch a mobile with footballs on it!

Nature versus nurture

For 2,500 years philosophers have argued the questions of what is nature and nurture, of innate versus acquired traits. The English philosopher John Locke (1632–1704) argued every child is born a 'tabula rasa', Latin for an empty slate. We are born blanks and everything we learn is inscribed on that.

One of the attractions of Locke's theory is that it implies we are all born equal. Your heredity can't make you more intelligent as everything is learned. So if we learned how to nurture children perfectly, we would soon have perfect children. A splendid delusion, Spelke argues. She is proud to be more in the nature than in the nurture camp and denies her core system theory is somehow threatening because it suggests that some people might be innately smarter than others. One must be cautious about any such claims of superiority, she warns, and adds 'you have to be very careful about what data you use'. Some data is tainted by cultural issues, she warns.

Be a man – talk like a child

Some fathers find it hard to talk to little children because to talk to a toddler, you have to be willing to talk slowly, and often childishly. You baby-talk to babies.

My friend Keesup denies he is inhibited about being childish. He regularly walks his daughter Scherezade to school in Pimlico. They talk and talk which he loves. 'I love the language which is charming and original,' he says. He knows this is a fleeting moment of learning. 'By the time she's seven she'll speak just like an adult.' He will miss the charm of her only half-formed language because much of it now is so inventive.

Language differentiates us from all other species. All parents wait for their child's first words. Some babies as young as nine months say something meaningful; Reuben said 'buff', for example, when he saw something that moved whether it was a car, bike or plane. On the other hand, Einstein said virtually nothing until he was four years old, so you need not panic if your toddler doesn't speak much at first.

Attempts to teach chimps sign language shows that the best they can achieve are utterances like that of a slow two-year-old who can say 'Me banana . . . want'. Noam Chomsky of MIT argues the expression 'learning to speak' is misleading. We learn but do not learn to speak. Human brains are hard-wired for language. In right handers, the crucial brain areas responsible for language have long been known to be in the left temporal lobe.

There is a very famous case in the history of language research which shows that the brain is a time sensitive machine. The 'wild child' of Aveyron in France was found in 1798 and local villagers believed the boy, who crawled on all fours and could only grunt, had been reared by wolves. The boy was taken to a Dr Itard who brought the boy to live with him and tried day and night to teach him to speak. He failed. A moving film, *L'Enfant Sauvage*, about the 'case' was made by Francois Truffaut. In the nineteenth century an Indian missionary called Singh found two 'wolf' children, but also did not manage to get them to speak normally.

A child who has lived isolated from human society and who has not learned to speak by the age of eight will not acquire normal language.

It isn't just these tragic cases that suggest language is innate. Chomsky showed all languages share what he called a 'deep structure' because we have an innate capacity to speak like we have an innate capacity to walk. So we do not learn to speak in a way that fits the normal laws of learning (Chomsky, 1957, 1986). If these laws worked with speech, children would just utter combinations of words they had already heard. But children do not only repeat words or sentences parents 'teach' them. Children produce original sentences, new combinations of words. 'The learning of language is creative', Chomsky told me in an interview (Cohen, 1977).

Fathers only have to listen to realise how true that is. Quite often children come out with strange sound combinations and, sometimes, they do just 'create', as a girl called Helen did when seeing a walrus at the zoo. She lay down on the grass, threw herself from one side to the other, and said 'flip flop . . . like a walrus'. A good description, but this combination of 'flip flop' and 'walrus' was not one she could ever have heard before.

Language may be innate but what parents do still matters. Parents teach children crucial skills involved in talking. You cannot have a conversation without giving and receiving non-verbal cues. When adults converse, they sense the rhythm of the talk, they pause to let others have a word, they 'leak' non-verbal cues to indicate, for example, that they are coming to the end of what they are saying.

As Keesup said of his daughter, and as I found, babies seem to enjoy 'chatting', even if all this is is gurgling at them. You may be saying nothing more meaningful that 'Ooe ee diddy daddy me' but the baby will pick up the rhythm of the sounds – which are the rhythms of speech.

Children whose parents talk to them, repeat things for them and explain the meaning of new words will have a better vocabulary younger. Yu and Smith tried to teach 28 12- to 14-month-olds six words by showing them two objects at a time on a computer monitor while two pre-recorded words were read to them. The tots got no hint about which word went with which image. After viewing various combinations of words and images, however, the children were surprisingly successful at figuring out which word went with which picture. Yu and Smith suggest that the more words tots hear, and the more information available for any individual word, the better the brain can begin to put together word–object pairings, so children learn more about the outside world (Yu and Smith, 2008).

Language learning is a nice example of how nurture and nature work together. Your children will benefit if you speak to them, read to them and play verbal games with them.

Language is not the only crucial test of humanity. So is being able to recognise yourself in the mirror. Some great apes can do that and there is some research which shows dolphins also behave differently when they see their own reflection as against that of other dolphins.

One of my editors reports that from the age of six months, her baby Annabel smiled at herself in the mirror and seemed to love it. But did Annabel know it was her?

"But daddy can be interactive, too."

Source: www.CartoonStock.com

10

Sex and personality

The Greeks, 2,000 years ago, argued that people were basically either calm or fiery. It is odd to find ancient Greek personality theory back in favour. Does the newborn tend to stay still or does he or she explore? Is the baby placid or nervous? One test is the 'tiger' test in which a man in a tiger mask appears. Does the baby cry, touch the tiger or just watch? Some optimists argue you need nothing else to work out a child's personality.

In the late 1950s, a major study looked at how children's personalities developed from birth on. Alexander Thomas and Stella Chess (Chess and Thomas, 1986) reported, 'children show distinct individuality in temperament in the first weeks of life, independently of their parents' handling or personality style'. They argued that the temperaments of babies were based on biology and were either 'easy, difficult, or slow to warm up'.

'Easy' babies responded well to various kinds of childrearing styles; 'difficult' babies had what the researchers called 'handling problems' from the beginning – no matter what their parents did. 'Slow to warm up' babies just seemed to take longer because they were 'slow'. They had low activity levels, withdrew from new experiences, were slow to adjust to change, and often had negative moods.

There's something to be said for slow because babies who love exploring get into scrapes and, sometimes, into real danger. I said you can't protect your child from everything. When Nicholas was nine months old, we went to spend Xmas with my in-laws who lived in Upper Saddle

River, New Jersey, in a rather grand house. Aileen was the oldest of six, her younger brothers and sisters loved the family dog.

One morning, Nicholas searched underneath the dining room table for a piece of cake; he didn't realise that his grandparents' dog was also scrabbling for scraps. Nicholas got the cake but the dog got Nicholas' nose. The dog was annoyed at having to fight for scraps he thought were his. The dog had bitten before, but all the children in the family were scared he would be put down. So they never told their parents the dog was dangerous.

Nicholas was rushed to hospital, had to have plastic surgery and spent his first Christmas among desperately sick children. He was put in a straitjacket to stop him scratching the skin graft off his nose. Once the emergency was over, Aileen and I realised we were lucky. At worst, Nicholas would have a bad scar. The other children kept in hospital over the holiday were desperately sick or dying. The ward was tense with fear, tense with parents trying to give their kids something nice at a Christmas which might be their last.

Five months later, undaunted, our son clambered into the oven of the cooker in the villa we had rented in Spain. We were in the living room and heard him scream. He had managed to pull the cooker down on top of himself. Miraculously, he was not hurt.

Schmidt and Fox distinguish between exuberant and inhibited children. Nicholas' readiness to explore meant he would score high on the exuberant side of the 'exuberance inhibition' scale. It seems to be a useful tool with children as young as four months of age (Schmidt and Fox, 1998).

Infants who are inhibited become fearful and do not explore seem to have a different physiology. First, their heart rate is relatively high but it does not change much if they are challenged. Second, these children have higher levels than average of the 'stress hormone' norepinephrine. In the mornings they also have high levels of cortisol.

Third, brain scans show that these 'inhibited' children seem to have more activity in the right-hand side of the brain. It has been claimed that this is linked to the amygdala, a structure in the cortex. Whole books have been written on the amygdala so I have to put it very basically. If the amygdala is more active, people feel more fear. The more active the amygdala is, the more likely the infant is to be fearful and so less likely to explore freely.

In *The Work of the Imagination* (2000), Harris reports that people who don't show an increased heart rate, when they read a text from a thriller, score lower on tests of reasoning and logic than do people who show strong physical and emotional reactions to such tales. There is some logic. The inhibited child who explores less learns less.

Dads, if you dive under the seat at the horror movie because you're so scared the vampire is going to bite you, you're very bright. Neither Einstein nor Freud went to horror movies. Now we know why – they would have been terrified out of their very brainy skulls.

More seriously dads have to tune in to the personality of their children. Jerome Kagan, a well known developmental psychologist, suggests 'the child's own temperamental predispositions are the major determining factors in the kind of person he becomes later in life' (Kagan, 1994). And these dispositions owe a lot to heredity but not everything.

Kagan suggests mothers and fathers need to recognise that each child has a unique personality. Getting to know your infant and how she or he approaches the world is, he argues, the most important parenting obligation.

- Parents should match their baby's personality. Every child needs a different approach. Think of special experiences designed with your baby's personality in mind. For example, if your baby is shy, create 'exploration' times to challenge her. If your baby is aggressive, set clear limits for acceptable behaviour. If your baby is fearful, help her find coping methods (playing with a favourite toy, singing a special song) that work for the both of you.
- Parents need to be flexible. Your child's personality will develop for years and that is bound to change your relationship with him or her.

- Whatever the changes of personality, children are stuck with their dads and mums. As a father try to be consistent and stable, in addition to flexible.

Erikson

For me, the psychiatrist who provides the best framework within which to understand research on personality during childhood is Erik Erikson (1902–1994). He worked at Harvard's Medical School and Psychological Clinic and he also spent a year observing Sioux children.

Erikson argued that young children make – or have made for them – key choices at particular stages and that these choices develop certain strengths. The stages are:

1. Infancy: Birth to 18 months
   Trust vs mistrust
   A question of drive and hope

Erikson also called infancy the Oral Sensory Stage – well, babies do put everything in the mouth. If mum and dad provide love, comfort and touching, the baby will learn to trust other people and have basic confidence in the future. If the baby is constantly frustrated as needs aren't met, the baby 'learns' consciously and unconsciously to distrust the world and that he is not worth much. The healthy baby learns to face the world with hope and drive.

2. Early childhood: 18 months to 3 years
   Autonomy vs shame
   A question of self control, courage and will

Erikson, like Piaget, stressed the child's need to master skills. The baby must learn to walk, talk, eat and interact with others in order to become a happy competent child. Mastering such basics builds our sense of self esteem and autonomy. Erikson made much of one ability toddlers learn during the 'Terrible Twos' (as he called them) – the ability to say 'NO!' And keep saying no. It may irritate parents but the child who never says no is likely to end up something of a victim later, Erikson claimed. He also claimed that if parents shamed a child during toilet training, the child learns shame, doubt and low self esteem.

3. Play age: 3 to 5 years
Initiative vs guilt
A question of purpose

Erikson argued that play is vital. It is a way of testing the world and our place in it. Toddlers play with dolls, trains, guns, each other. In the chapter on pretending, it becomes clear how that is crucial. Play teaches a child initiative. Erikson stressed the stages of sexual development less than Freud did and the stages of intellectual development less than Piaget did, but he did believe in Freud's Oedipal conflict to some extent. He believed that the best way for children to resolve that was through 'social role identification', doing things dads did and playing with dad. The child who does not manage to play and to identify with his parents is likely to suffer guilt.

4 School age: 6 to 12 years
Industry vs inferiority
A question of method and competence

Well adjusted children should be able to learn and work. They should also develop social skills and make friends. Erikson talked of having a sense of industry. Children who don't manage that know that they are not good enough and so harbour feelings of inadequacy and inferiority. They are likely to suffer practically because they will have serious problems of competence, and psychologically, because they will have chronically low self esteem.

Erikson did not argue that babies 'choose'. Heredity and environment, what parents deal them and how they deal with what their parents deal them, make the choices. Free will does exist, he thought, because he saw and studied many individuals who gave up and gave in, but also many others who fought and struggled against all odds. Fates are not fixed. Life is a series of challenges. We need to rise to them. Or partly rise. Biology matters but sheer bloody mindedness also helps.

Apologies for sounding like a self help zealot. But sometimes psychologists forget about our human ability to change by just deciding that is what we will do. Erikson seemed more aware of that than most shrinks.

The nanny state

There is a real political issue about whether the state should help teach people to be better parents. Part of me says 'of course if it helps children'. Part of me is more sceptical. The psychoanalyst D.W. Winnicott argued many mothers worried they were inadequate mothers. They wanted to be perfect mothers who would perfectly and totally meet all their child's needs. Obsession lies that way, he warned.

But there are so many instances of neglected and abused children that it is understandable governments feel they have to do something. In Britain and America we have seen programmes set up for men so that they can improve as fathers. They seem to do something at least for some but not all fathers – and no one is too sure whether or not the improvement lasts.

In Philadelphia, Jay Fagan set up a pilot father programme based around local Head Start groups and showed it helped fathers as well as their children. Mothers' attitudes changed when they saw once useless fathers blossom into 'competent caregivers, play partners, and nurturing but firm disciplinarians' (Fagan and Iglesias, 1999). But it is not easy to keep fathers really involved for long (McBride, Bae and Rane, 2001).

Being a good father is not rocket science but it does need love and attention to detail. I once wrote a book about Mrs Beeton, the Victorian cook, who also offered mothers advice on childcare, as well as on how to sack a dishonest butler.

As I re-read her book, I was astonished how sound, to use that Victorian word, Mrs Beeton's advice on childcare was. Children had to be kept clean, well fed and busy. Hygiene was the root of all good. A child needed a clean room, good food – breast or bottle at the right time at the right temperature – and properly mashed purées once baby had been weaned. Mrs Beeton suggested more oxtail and oysters than nutritionists would now, but she was keen on a balanced diet 150 years ago.

The psychological needs of children are not strange either. A child needs:

attention
affection, cuddling is good
the chance to grasp and manipulate objects
the chance to play with other children
the chance to explore
the chance to be listened to
freedom from violence, sexual abuse and neglect
emotional security.

Give these things to a child and that child will feel loved. If you give your baby the essentials on the list, you will be, not the perfect father, but a good enough dad.

The child who feels loved and safe will have the self confidence to test what the world is like because he, or she, knows they can scamper quickly back to the safety of home, to Bowlby's 'secure base' which was discussed in the chapter on bonding. Fathers play a large role in creating that self confidence.

Happy memories for dad at least

I will always remember walking through Greenwich Park with Nicholas when I was taking him to nursery school. For 30 minutes, we talked as we made our way past the deer park, past the oak which had been planted in Elizabeth I's reign and past the boating pond. I don't remember what we talked about but it was lovely and we didn't run out of chat. I enjoyed every minute of it.

At about 8.30 a.m, we would get to Nicholas's Montesorri school. If I didn't have to rush to work I waited till the school opened but sometimes I just had to go. As soon as one of the mothers I knew – and it was nearly always a mother – arrived, I asked if she minded taking Nicholas in. Sometimes, he cried as I left and, then, I explained I really had to get my train and I went.

We walked this walk most kindergarten days for three years. Was this perfect fathering? Of course not. The perfect father would have stayed, missed his train, been late for work, coped with the work–life stresses Norwegian fathers complain about. Was it good enough fathering? I would say yes. I never left him alone, never left him with an adult I did not know, and never left without explaining to him why I had to catch the train.

Being a good enough father, however, will not protect your children from everything. I have already described the saga of Nicholas' nose and of the oven. The third accident we had to deal with was Reuben's broken arm when he was 11. He was practising karate chops on a mattress and his arm snapped. I will now demonstrate how dads can take pride in the most bizarre 'achievements' of their children. After it was clear the arm would heal and that Reuben would not be disabled in any way, the surgeon said it had been very unusual. Reuben had a hole in his bone in the upper arm. A new technique had been used to fix it. Our son's arm would be the subject of a learned paper in a medical journal. My son, I don't just love him, but his arm has made medical history.

Don't try to be a perfect father. You'll make mistakes. You'll feel angry. You'll wish your adorable little monkey/demanding kid would stop crying in the middle of the night. You'll yell for them to shut up. It's no good pretending that sometimes your child drives you mad. Inevitably there will be times when your son or daughter exasperates you; the test for any father is how he deals with that.

But always remember how unequal the relationship is between you, the powerful parent, and the weak, dependent child. Stay in control of your feelings. Your child should never have to cope with your bad moods. That's easy to say but it can require great self discipline. Fathers need that and in later chapters dealing with anger management, I offer advice on how to achieve that self discipline.

11

The toddler's brain

Pour yourself a glass of wine in a long stemmed glass up to a line you have marked.

Don't touch a drop.

Now pour the contents of that glass into a fat tumbler.

Pour some more wine into the long stemmed glass again up to that line.

It seems ridiculous to ask which of the two full glasses holds more wine. But the Swiss child psychologist Jean Piaget based much of his theory of how the toddler's brain developed on a rather similar experiment. As Piaget's work remains so influential, it needs to be covered in detail.

Between two and seven, Piaget claimed, the child still cannot master logical operations and so he called this the 'preoperational' stage. It was defined by the fact that children until they are about seven are totally egocentric.

Piaget did not use the term 'egocentric' to mean being totally selfish or self obsessed. Preoperational children were centred on themselves or egocentric, as they couldn't imagine how anything might look from anyone else's perspective; they were slaves to the 'here and now' because they could not hold alternatives in their mind.

The conservation task was one of Piaget's classic experiments though he used water rather than wine. He showed six-year-old children Container A which was filled with water to a certain level. Then he would pour the water out of Container A and into Container B while the children watched. Nothing was hidden but Container B was thinner and longer than the first. Then came the crunch question. Was there more or less water in B than there was in A, Piaget would ask.

Children younger than seven nearly always replied there was more water in Container B even though they had seen the identical water poured from Container A. Not a drop was spilled. Piaget saw this as proof that children were trapped by their immediate perceptions. Container B looks as if it has more water than Container A but children under seven can't remember precisely what was in Container A; so they say there is more water in Container B. Piaget coined the term 'abusive perceptions' to describe this; pre-operational children were victims of those.

There is a difference between Piaget's experiment and the wine glass game I started with. Piaget's children did not look at both containers when they had water in them. But the evidence on baby memory suggests young children should not be confused because they cannot remember what is in the containers.

Then, Piaget found something else. When children were asked to perform the container task after they were six years old, they often became uneasy. Piaget suggested that the children were becoming anxious. They began to sense their view of the world was not quite right; it was primitive, illogical. They felt what Piaget called 'disequilibrium'. Equilibrium would not be restored until they had stopped being pre-operational and, then, the container task would seem totally obvious. But are four year olds really as naïve as Piaget suggested? We will return to the question after discussing what was once a political hot potato – IQ.

Another Piaget game

As with hiding your child's toys, Piaget's study is not hard to replicate. Do the container experiment with your child when they are five, six and seven years old. Jot down what they say – and see how it makes them laugh when they are eight years old.

Paris 1903 – the birth of IQ

Psychologists have been studying children's IQ for over a century. Today British schools are supposed to identify especially bright kids but some teachers resist that – and that's interesting because the history of IQ is linked to that of education.

Many Parisian children were doing poorly at school so the city asked two French psychologists, Alfred Binet and Theodore Simon, to find out how to help them. The somewhat quaint tasks they devised for children – four-year-olds, for example, were given instructions to follow; they were told to pick up a key, put it on a chair at one end of the room, shut a door, then pick up a box and bring it back to the experimenter – became the basis of all subsequent IQ tests.

The children had to carry out a sequence of five actions. Most four-year-olds could not manage that but half the five-year-olds did. Six-years-olds did better.

The average six-year-old could manage to:

- tell the difference between morning and evening
- copy the picture of a diamond
- count 13 pennies
- distinguish between pictures of ugly and pretty faces.

The average eight-year-old could manage to:

- compare two objects from memory
- count up to 20 without hesitation
- say what had been left out of a picture he had just seen
- repeat back a list of five digits.

Questions of this kind are the basis of all IQ tests – and there are hundreds of different varieties. Nearly all Simon and Binet's questions had a definite right or wrong answer; the only one that allowed some wiggle room was the one about telling a pretty from an ugly face. Once they had discovered what was normal for children of different ages, they measured how well a particular child did.

It's important to grasp that the IQ test is a comparative measure, not an absolute one. If I weigh 76 kilos that is an absolute measure. I may be light or heavy for my age and height but the 76 kilos is 76 kilos.

IQ scores are relative. They compare a child with the average for his group. IQ is not some magical fixed entity.

Binet and Simon gave 20 questions. After a while, they concluded that the norm for six-year-olds was to be able to answer 12 of these questions. A six-year-old who answered 12 out of the 20 questions correctly would have an IQ of 100, dead average. So Binet and Simon created the following equation:

The intelligence quotient is:
Mental age divided by Chronological age × 100

Binet and Simon's norm for nine-year-olds was to get 18 questions right. The six-year-old child who got the right answers to all the questions a nine-year-old should would achieve an IQ score of:

$9/6 = 1.5 \times 100 = 150$

Research from 1903 to 1960 showed that only 4 children in 1,000 have an IQ of above 140. Einstein's IQ has been reckoned at above 180. One woman has recently been found to have an IQ that yo-yoes between 187 and 226 depending on her mood, the time of day and other factors.

Psychologists went on to claim there was a factor of general intelligence called 'G'. In the 1980s, American psychologists like Robert Ornstein, Robert Sternberg and Howard Gardner argued that, while a factor of general intelligence underlies all mental abilities, there are more specialised intelligences. Ornstein called them 'modules' in the mind and they would seem to be much like Spelke's 'cores'.

We should recall Jerome Kagan's advice to adapt to your child's personality. For fathers, should also adapt to their kind of intelligence. If you really want to understand your child, you need to get to know his or her strengths and weaknesses, the modules of their mind. Long before Spelke's work, psychologists established that there are many different kinds of intelligence – verbal, numerical, spatial, practical, musical, social, emotional intelligences all matter. She might call them cores now; they tended to call them 'modules'. A quick guide to the main ones follows.

Verbal intelligence

Those who score high on that will find crosswords, anagrams and other verbal games and puzzles easy and fun. They will like rhyming games. They can rejig the letters that make the word PATERNAL to make PARENTAL. They will know without thinking that these words rhyme with RENTAL; DENTAL and MENTAL and, though the spelling is different, GENTLE.

We live in a very verbal culture. Exams depend not just on what you know but how you can say it. Verbal intelligence correlates highly with school and exam results. But 20 per cent of adults are 'functionally illiterate', according to a British report by Sir Claus Moser (1998). The figure rises to nearly 40 per cent in some areas. The government has spent millions on advertising campaigns which try to get adults who can't read to seek help. Some of these campaigns betray, I fear, the way we look down on those who are not literate. I am not sure that saying people have 'gremlins' helps, especially as a number of ads for toilet cleaners trumpet the fact that Boggo will destroy the germs in your loo which is crawling with creatures who look much like the gremlins in the literacy ads. It remains worrying that in a country where people love gardening, more than 10 per cent of a sample were unable to read the instructions on a packet of seeds.

Numerical intelligence

Many children start playing on computers very young, many have poor numerical skills. The Basic Skills Agency found in 1996 that only 20 per cent of Britons could solve

12 simple mathematical questions like $5 - 1.78 =$, or $14 \times 11 =$, correctly.

In 2003, the UK Department for Education found that 29 per cent of adults, some 11 million people, could not calculate the area of a floor, in either square feet or metres. Less than a third managed to work out the amount of plastic covering needed to line a pond – even with a calculator, pen and paper.

I don't recommend that dads try to turn their children into calculating machines but you could, when they are young, play number games with them. One is to put three Smarties in one hand and two in the other. Your toddler can have all of them if he adds up how many there are.

Spatial intelligence

This 'core' is the ability to understand spatial relationships so that you can see that if you rotate a figure through 90 degrees it will look quite different.

If you notice that your child is not very good with shapes, you can buy jigsaws and do them together. The art and science of fathering is all about playing and eventually playing useful games with your kids.

Practical intelligence

We all know people who can pass exams and do the theory but are hopelessly impractical. Ask them to assemble a do-it-yourself desk or other furniture and they fall apart. I have seen intelligent men (i.e. me) driven to distraction by trying to assemble a DIY book shelf. I plan to write a paper on 'Sadism and Self Assembly Furniture'. Those who design it are sadists; those who buy it knowing they'll never be able to build it are either masochists or trying to repent for all kinds of guilt.

Social intelligence

This is the ability to deal with other people and to understand their motives. There are some connections between this and the now fashionable concept of 'emotional intelligence'.

Howard Gardner has stressed that some children with poor verbal and social skills nevertheless show enormous talent in painting and drawing.

The biology of G – the general factor of intelligence

Recent results, however, have made some neuroscientists stress general rather than specific intelligence, and its cores again. American researchers led by Jeremy Gray have found that subjects who score high on a much used IQ test, *Raven's Advanced Progressive Matrices*, show more activity in specific brain regions when they do memory tests. Differences in brain activity correlate with how well, or badly, individuals do; these differences show up in the lateral prefrontal cortex, an area associated with memory, planning and goal-directed activity. Those with high IQ got distracted less when the experimenters tried to distract them. Gray asked his subjects to look at a series of words or pictures of faces on a computer screen. They then had to say whether each word or picture was the same as one presented two, three, four or five screens before. Those with high IQ scores had better memory and showed greater brain activity.

For dads the question is – what can you do to keep your toddler alert and their brain active? The answer is play, talk, interact. Do not veg out too much in front of the telly.

You will soon notice if your child talks well, sings well, if they have a sense of how Lego™ fits together. Be open to their intellectual individuality. Be ready to spend time doing things they are really interested in.

If you see a problem (i.e. if your child has a poor vocabulary or is really clumsy), you can spend time on activities that are remedial but don't seem remedial. Who said parents never cheat? You just have to cheat subtly. It's a question of not being too obvious. Do not say you are going to teach your kid, but spend time doing things that seem to be fun and are fun, but fun with a purpose – to help fix a particular problem and give your child the confidence to face it.

Most four- and five-year-olds are canny and can sense what parents are trying to do and resent it. Older children can be even more defensive, so you have to be sly, fly and not let a battle of wills develop. But spend time on things your child finds hard and do it routinely, not just when it has become an issue because he or she has failed at something.

Vitamins and intelligence

Diet affects the brain. Children whose nutrition is poor when very young are likely to have lower than average IQ scores, though it's hard to be sure malnutrition is the only cause as deprived children are usually deprived in a number of ways. But there is one persuasive study. A group of 30 Welsh children were given a vitamin and mineral supplement every day; at the end of eight months, they had gained an average of 10 points on a non-verbal IQ test while a control group who just got more attention only gained 2–4 points. There was enormous publicity (Benton and Roberts, 1988). The late Hans Eysenck, author of many books on IQ, told me that he was amazed by how strong the evidence was for the benefits of vitamins, especially vitamin C. Some psychologists thought he was too enthusiastic. Professor N.J. Mackintosh, of Cambridge University, for example, warned that 'legitimate doubts will not be dispelled until specific predictions (who will benefit, on what test, from what sort of supplementation) have been formulated and tested properly' (Mackintosh, 1999).

Jamie Oliver in his Channel 4 series *School Dinners* fastened on to a related issue. Is he the Mrs Beeton of our times? Children need good food, not junk food. Small amounts of extra vitamins and minerals may not be a magic potion but, used sensibly, they won't do any harm. Blueberries are probably best as pointed out earlier.

It is easy for parents to get obsessed about their child's IQ, but it's not particularly intelligent for a number of reasons.

IQ tests only test one particular kind of intelligence. They tell you nothing about imagination, or creativity. Second, children come under pressure at school soon enough. In 2008, the United Nations criticised the UK for testing children more than any other country. Third, there is no evidence that having a high IQ predicts a great future.

Eysenck, who was very positive about intelligence and personality tests, told me he had noticed that many members of MENSA (an organisation that you can only join if you have an IQ of 140 or above) were neither particularly rich nor particularly successful. Their main and, often only, claim to fame was having a high IQ. At first Eysenck was rather disappointed, but I have a sneaking suspicion that he eventually was tickled pink that the great achievement in life of many MENSA members was to manage to get into MENSA (Cohen, 1994).

IQ is necessary but not sufficient – and it is not that necessary. To do well in life you need personality, persistence, other modes of thinking. If you are really anxious that your child is slow or falling behind in class, you should take your child to an educational psychologist for a rounded assessment. DIY testing is not usually that reliable.

A thousand books

Dads who want to help their kids read to them – and there are more and, arguably, better and brighter books for children than ever before, though some classics like the Dr Seuss books are magic still. Keesup Choe told me that he started reading to his daughter when she was three months old as he put her to bed. He still reads to her at night time now that she is six years old. Never mind whether it is educational which he knows perfectly well that it is. It's also fun.

One of the reasons Dr Seuss works so well is that most children love rhymes and there is much research which links readiness to read with the ability to make and understand rhymes.

One game fathers can play with their children is the rhyming game. All you need do is spend five to ten minutes an evening on questions like this which you can put to your children – and laugh with them about.

1 Which kind of tea do you want for your bee?
   • Bee Tea
   • Flea Tea
   • Wee Tea (which children will love because it is rude)
2 What animal rhymes with clog?
3 Which part of the body rhymes with sand?
4 Complete the following verse:
       You'll get me mad
       If you spit on . . .
Answers to (2) include dog.
Answers to (3) include hand.
Answers to (4) include dad.

Dads have to be willing to be totally childish. And this is an excellent time to get the camera or video. Don't miss out. Take pictures of your children, show them to them and talk about the pictures with your small kids. No research proves what effect this will have, but it is likely to help you bond – especially if dad is wearing an absurd hat and making silly faces.

Self Analysis 7
Ask yourself:
How childish are you willing to be?
What worries you about being childish?
Have you thought of discussing making a complete idiot of yourself with your partner?
If you have not, do so now.

And that starts from nursery school on.

Choosing a good nursery

Aileen and I found choosing a good nursery simple. Our friends downstairs had sent their children to Miss Sayer who ran a Montessori nursery behind St Alfege's Church in Greenwich. Nicholas thrived there. We paid about £30 a month. Wonderful value but Miss Sayer had a friend who was vastly rich and we all suspected he backed the school. Today the government is committed to providing nursery school places for most children aged two or more.

As a result, there are standards which should make it easier for parents to check they are entrusting their child to a proper childminder or nursery. Childminders have to be registered in the UK. Crèches and childminders who provide services for children aged under two should have no more than 12 children in their care. Half the staff should have received training, but the guidelines do not specify what kind of training. There should be at least one carer for every three children under the age of two and one for every four children aged two. There need only be one member of staff to every eight children for children aged between three and five.

It's important to ask questions. A key one is about staff turnover because small children need stability.

Ask: how often does the staff change?

The law does allow nurseries to include regular unpaid volunteers among the number of carers but ask how many are volunteers who could leave at any moment.

Ask about the experience of the person in charge. You do not want to discover they worked in the City till they got the sack in the great economic squeeze.

Ask about how they plan the activities of the babies. There should be time to rest but also plenty of opportunities for play.

Check there is a separate area where babies can sleep while others are playing. Also check there is a safe outdoor playing space.

When your child is being looked after by others, play close attention to how they are at home. If they are suddenly secretive or seem scared, ask why.

Nicholas' experiences at Miss Sayer's made me a modest fan of the Montessori system. Maria Montessori believed in play and learning through play. I don't say that Montessori nurseries are the best, but they tend to be good. Most of them charge but many of the criteria I have argued parents should check apply to state-funded nursery schools too.

When they were at nursery school, my children certainly learned three key skills – how to play, how to use their imagination and, yes, how to tell fibs.

12

Lies, games and the imagination – oh, and the small matter of big dragons: how children don't lie brilliantly

Sigmund Freud might have been on to something in 1908 when he wrote that 'every child at play behaves like a creative writer, in that he creates a world of his own'. Writers make up characters and so do children. Writers also make up imaginary worlds like Tolkien's Middle Earth – and so do children. Some psychologists wonder why and how most adults lose the gift of imagination. Freud believed that as the child was trained to become a good member of society, the capacity for fancy was lost. Except for a few artists.

Children today live in an utterly different world from that which Freud and Piaget grew up in. They are exposed through the media to information, influences and games in a way that developmental psychology is only slowly mastering. Karen Bartsch, an authority on how small children think, told me that toddlers also interact more socially than ever before. Kids go to day care, they don't live in nuclear families, they play more pretend play; they communicate with far more other people at younger ages than they did in the past.

In this chapter I want to offer fathers an introduction to the charming and complex research on how children pretend, lie and use their imaginations. It's an area that has intrigued me. I'd like to say it was because I did not have any play mates when I was small but, in fact, when I lived in Israel I loved playing with my older cousins Lydia and Anita. Whatever the reasons, I did my PhD on what makes children laugh, spent hours observing playgroups and then, in the early 1990s, I met Dr Stephen Mackeith who was a psychiatrist with a strange hobby – studying the imaginary worlds that some children devise. He had collected over 50 such case histories.

In much of this book I have reported research other people do. In this chapter, my own work is weaved in.

Children will start to pretend on the whole before they lie but since research on lying is fairly simple, I shall start with lying.

The earliest lies are denials. Ask a child if he has thumped his brother and he just says 'No'. Often children give themselves away by laughing nervously at the same time as they utter the lie. Stephen Ceci, professor at Cornell University, says that children do not like lying and, as a result, they allow their body language to betray them. Often, three- and four-year-olds place their hands in front of their mouth when fibbing. The symbolism is cute.

Some bit of conscience tells the child: hide your mouth! It's not speaking the truth.

Most five-years-olds are more subtle and realise the sharp mum or dad might notice! But many children still leak – the language in which body language research is phrased is very inelegant – non-verbal signals. They often look down at their feet and avoid all eye contact when they lie. We leak when we lie because we are not good at hiding the tension we feel when lying.

Lie for me, kid

Stephen Ceci claims children can get uncomfortable about lying even when the lie is a white lie. He told a conference I filmed that he had to take his five-year-old daughter to hospital to see her mother. Ceci told his daughter that if anyone asked her age, she was to say she was six years old. Children younger than that were not allowed to visit the sick.

Daughter and dad get in a lift. A nurse smiles at them and asks how old the little girl is.

'I'm five but he told me to say I was six,' says Ceci's daughter.

Ceci also set up situations in which his daughter had to lie to protect him though I am not sure how convincing the scenario of Ceci as a criminal was. She had seen him steal some toys and he told her she must not get him into trouble. On the film he made we see how uncomfortable his daughter became. She twitched, she hesitated to speak, she tried to avoid eye contact, she showed 'leakage'. But she did not betray her dad and tried to lie valiantly. For Ceci the lesson is clear. Children lie much like adults do but, on the whole, they are less skilful about it.

You think you are the great detective because you can spot when your children are lying. Ceci's work suggests that what you are really doing is responding to blatant cues and clues. And we shouldn't flatter ourselves we always know what the little darlings think.

Self Analysis 8
Ask yourself:
How do you react when you catch your child in a lie?
Do you get furious?
Do you try to explain why lying is wrong?
Do you think about the way your parents reacted when they caught you lying?
Can you remember your first lie?

Lord of the Flies

Anyone who has read William Golding's *Lord of the Flies* knows how brutal the games children play can become. A group of boys get marooned on a desert island. Within a few days, some become leaders and torture the weaker ones.

In a famous 'prison experiment' which inspired a BBC TV series, Philip Zimbardo, a Californian psychologist, divided students into prisoners and guards to see how they behaved. He had to stop the experiment after three days because the pretend guards were being so brutal to the pretend prisoners. He told me he could never do that

experiment now because there are so many ethical constraints on research (Cohen, 2005). Zimbardo's work showed
how easy it is to forget the boundaries between the real and
make believe. Yet children do learn this naturally. By the
age of four, most children know the limits. You can't hit
other children hard when playing because hitting someone
hard is not play. Play has boundaries.

The development of play

Thirty years ago two American psychologists, Curry and
Arnaud, made the following findings.

Two-year-olds played with toys, but did not play with
other children; they often imitated other children, but they
did not have the *social skills to play with them*. Small
toddlers just could not collaborate well enough to play
cowboys and Indians or cops and robbers.

Three-year-olds started to play with each other but
were very erratic.

Curry and Arnaud found that when the toddlers
reached the age of four then they started to play real
games together. They were well enough attuned to each
other; they knew what another child liked or hated so they
could play together (Curry and Arnaud, 1974).

They found three- and four-year-olds liked chases and
pretending to be often superheroes or monsters. But girls
did not play Superman. The boys played with guns, the
girls played with dolls. There is not much evidence to
suggest such play has changed and many psychologists
complain that too much play is rather sex-stereotyped.

Hello hello

In the Greenwich playground I observed how complex
pretending can be. Here's one scene. One boy pretends to
pour Daniel a cup from the kettle saying 'yes sir'. Daniel
giggles. Then he dives under the table in the Wendy House,
gets up, places a cup on his head and says 'Hello hello'. The
cup clatters on the table and he laughs. A moment later,
another boy pretends to pour tea from the kettle into a cup

and chuckles. He then feeds Jamie from the spout and he and Daniel laugh.

Scampering with dad on the floor making noises like an elephant is perfectly good play for both children and parents. It is an excellent way of bonding with your kid and de-stressing yourself after a tough day in the so-called real world.

Pretend play has become a hot topic in psychology because the ability to pretend enables children to learn many essential social and emotional skills. It also teaches that I am not the only person in the universe.

By the time they are 15 months old, most children will show some pretence. Psychologists like Lorraine McCune-Nicolich, Judy Dunn and Paul Harris have looked at the development of pretending since the 1980s. Most children will first pretend by carrying out an action where something vital is missing. Often, they pretend to eat even though there is no food. The child will lift an empty spoon up to his mouth and go 'yum yum', adding for effect mouth movements.

Alison Gopnik of the University of California, Berkeley, is at times almost lyrical, a rare quality in a contemporary psychologist. She imagines – and why should psychologists not be imaginative in studying imagination – that a toddler may first think 'Mum gave me this plastic duck because she wants me to play with it.' But, hey, a duck may be more than a duck and the toddler then soars into fairy land: 'This plastic duck is a magic swan that will fly me up to a cloud castle, where I'll be a princess.' Lyrical indeed.

Children master the idea of miming very young. They realise that to act out drinking, you don't need to have a cup. The mime is often accompanied by laughter. And with words that are imaginative. Gopnik (Gopnik *et al.*, 2001) noted babies who say 'apple' while pretending to eat a ball or 'night-night' while tucking a teddy bear into bed.

A normal 18-month-old will often pretend to feed another person or a doll. The child will put an empty spoon to the doll's mouth. First, the doll is just a passive recipient. But, then, most infants start to give the doll 'life'. The child now takes on two parts – that of the feeder and, almost like a ventriloquist, that of the doll. As the child feeds the doll the child also makes noises which reveal what the doll feels.

The doll who loves the food says 'yum'.

The doll who hates the food says 'yuck'.

I don't want to sound like Anatole le Obscure, some French philosopher, but there are complex issues here. Somehow the child who feeds a doll and makes yum or yuck sounds has mastered a very complex skill. I'll try and get into the mind of said kid. Said kid 'knows' he is the kid feeding the doll; said kid also 'knows' he can be at the same time the animated doll who says 'yuck' or 'yum'. It's really quite clever and, given that nearly all kids do it, it's a relief we don't have more cases of multiple personality disorder.

The earliest pretence with my children I saw was when Reuben was 18 months old. He ran around the living room yelling 'I'm Batman'. To add to the effect he draped a cape round his shoulders.

Did he realise what he was doing, I wondered. Was there a corner of his mind which knew perfectly well, as an actor or a six-year-old would, that he was not really Batman? I could not tell. But I had few doubts by the time he was three. I was sure he knew when he rushed about as Fantastic Man that really he was not truly this self-invented superhero. Reuben helped as he did explain when I asked him that sadly there were differences between himself and Fantastic Man; he couldn't really fly and didn't have Fantastic Man's magic powers.

Reuben was fascinated by Batman when he was two, and he worked the characters into his chases. Two months later on, he could imagine himself playing a part as he chased, smiling as he said 'Superman . . . I fly' and ran around the living room. He also often rushed round the room saying he was Aquaman or Fantastic Man. The most original character was as a flying cucumber; this aerodynamic vegetable held us spellbound as Reuben zoomed around the room.

The prestigious Max Planck Institute has reported research on pretend play (2005). The kinds of early games I have described the Planck-ites reveal 'can be considered as the first form of true collective intentionality in ontogeny – involving shared cooperative activities and even some rudimentary form of joint creation of status functions'. Well, now, you know the kind of language in which proper developmental psychology should be stated. I think this means that when toddlers play it is the first time they do things together – deliberately and with some kind of plan.

Teaching play

Fathers need to give time to playing with their children even when the children aren't research subjects. I was, at least, willing to appear a perfect idiot. Gaskins *et al.* (2007) reported that when children pretended with their caregivers, they played more complex, more elaborate and more extended games than when they pretended by themselves. The study added 'And they used the ideas that the parents initiated in their subsequent pretending.'

A child playing by himself may sit behind a toy steering wheel, turn it and make engine noises. A parent joining in can take the child on a pretend trip, teaching along the way. One of the things parents do when they do that is to introduce the child to their culture. They also found differences between Taiwan Chinese and white, middle-class Americans. The latter saw pretend play as a child-centred activity. The Chinese parents more often than not initiated play and used it to teach social customs or routines, like how to greet a guest or teacher.

For most fathers, taking part in pretend play seems 'very related to how much they enjoy it', the study concluded. For most mothers, though, it seems related to 'how important they feel it is to children's development'.

Tree therapy

Many men do find it hard to let go, to be silly because so much of our lives is devoted to being serious. Having a child gives you permission to play and there is the bonus of knowing that playing is actually likely to be good for your child. Learn to loosen up. Kids can be wonderful for that. I have already suggested that dads should lie on the floor and kick with their babies. When your child is a little older, play the tree game with him or her.

It does not require much to be a tree. Stick your arms out. Stay still.

Then make the dramatic announcement: 'I am a tree.'

Your kid may laugh but tell them they too have to be a tree. But you can both be talking trees who see what is around. You can be very old trees. As the older wiser tree dad can say all kinds of nonsense like 'I spy with my tree-eye some Neanderthals deep in the jungle.'

Look at yourself in the mirror and repeat 'It's sometimes good to be ridiculous.'

Santa Claus is half real

When little girls are toddlers, fathers can lark about with them as they do with boys but the time will come when your girl is too old to laugh at you playing the elephant – and you may not know how to play with dolls. This may be the time to learn new skills. One obvious thing you can do is to teach your kids, boys or girls, how to cook. You can play soldiers with your son and you can dress up dolls in historical costumes and play with them with your daughter.

Children seem to understand more than we used to imagine of what we might call 'the grammar of pretending'. Harris was also part of a group that studied how children understand pretending from the age of 17 months to 57 months (Kavanaugh and Harris, 2003). Some children got the idea as early as 18 months.

At 29 months of age, most children could understand the 'pretend framework'. If experimenters poured pretend tea over a duck, children of that age would say the duck was wet though no tea had been poured and the duck was totally dry. The children got the game and the grammar of the game. So, they said, the duck was now wet. A few months later, the children realised that, just as they could pretend, a doll could also pretend the duck was wet. The children could even make a doll pretend. It is strange, given that society sees pretending as silly, that it seems to be vital for cognitive and social development. Somewhere between three and four years of age, the child who can play the ordinary pretend games I've described makes a quantum leap.

Harris recently did a nice study in which he showed a three-year-old the boy a box and asked him to imagine that a monster lived inside. The boy had no trouble doing that but he knew how nervous psychologists are and he reassured Harris that it was all make believe and that a monster would not really pop out if they opened the box. Especially as they see so much media, small children become savvy about shades of fantasy.

Woolley and her associates (Sharon and Woolley, 2004) claimed that children have surprisingly subtle conceptions of fantasy creatures. A majority of three- to five-year-olds strongly believed in Santa Claus and the Easter Bunny, but many children hedged a bit, saying they were not sure or did not know whether fantasy creatures such as dragons and fairies actually exist.

Young children may have a 'kind of real' category for thinking about fantastic entities, Woolley argues. And they also learn something great conmen have known for centuries.

Make 'em laugh, make 'em laugh

Without anyone telling them, many children discover a very adult skill – that if you make someone laugh you can sometimes get away, well, not with murder but with quite a lot of bad behaviour. I saw this in my own children when they were aged between two and three years. But I was far from the first to see it. The British psychologist James Sully saw his son aged 2 years and a month often try to get away with bad behaviour by laughing. The young Sully 'began to show himself a veritable rebel against parental authority'. He would sometimes hit his parents and 'follow up the sacrilege with a profane laugh' (Sully, 1912). Nicholas was a fellow naughty spirit.

When Nicholas was 3 years 9 months, he often devised games to delay going to sleep. First, he would try a simple no. 'I won't', he said and laughed at me. Then, he put his pyjama top the wrong way round quite on purpose. He laughed again, put his trousers on and span round like a top. 'Stop it,' I said. 'It's funny,' he insisted.

Nicholas was as capable of 'sacrilege' as the young Sully was. He often laughed when he knew he was annoying or defying me by putting coins in his mouth, brushing his brother's toes with his toothbrush and other rebellious acts. Sometimes, he was really funny and I found it hard not to laugh. Once he toothbrushed his brother's feet and was convinced, in all his three-year-old wisdom, he would get away with it more easily if he made me laugh.

My child is a real person – what do I do now?

Between three and five years of age, children discover other people have other ideas, other feelings and, what philosophers call 'other minds', a sense of other people. I am not you, you are not me. In 36 short months, they have grown from 'buzzing blooming confusion' to an almost person.

Psychologists have looked at when small children start to talk about believing, hoping, liking, wanting, what are technically called mental states. A mental state cannot be observed. It is inside your mind. It is revealed by what children say and do; for example, when infants begin to use verbs that reflect mental states. When a toddler says 'I want', 'I think', 'I believe', 'I wish', 'I dream', 'I like' and so on, we assume that he or she is expressing the fact they're experiencing the relevant mental state of wanting, believing or dreaming.

At the University of Michigan, Henry Wellman and Karen Bartsch have analysed some 200,000 conversations between children, parents and other adults (Bartsch and Wellman, 1995). To parents, many of the conversations with four-year-olds that Wellman and Bartsch record will feel familiar. Here is a dialogue in which ages with full stops (i.e. 3.10) indicate years and months (i.e. 3 years and 10 months).

Ross (3.10):   Leslie makes me angry.
Adult: Why?

Ross: If she thinks something is silly. I don't think it's
    silly at all.
Adult: Oh, you had a disagreement.
Ross: Uh huh, she thought her necklace was silly.
Adult: She thought it was silly?
Ross: Yeah. But I didn't think it was.

Ross understands Leslie has a mind of her own, and what
Leslie is thinking is not what Ross is thinking. When the
adult asks tough questions, Ross explains the situation
competently that he and Leslie disagree about the necklace.

I wish, I want, I like, I think

Children talked of desires from when they were just 18
months. Eve and Mark, both aged 18 months, were the first
to use expressions like 'I want'. But the talk soon got complex. Abe (2.5) heard his mother ask his father if he enjoyed
the cranberry muffin. The boy said 'I wanna a cranberry
muffin. I like them.' This is, of course, a psychological
explanation; Abe wants a cranberry muffin because he likes
them. Most three-year-olds could talk about wishes and
desires in a 'correct' way.

   About 1 in every 40 utterances had to do with wishes
while only 1 in 120 utterances concerned thoughts or
beliefs. Nevertheless, by the age of 3 years and 5 months
every child had said something about beliefs.

   Rather more to their surprise Wellman and Bartsch
found some children began to talk about thinking when
they are very young. One dialogue shows that.

   Adam (2.11):   I . . . just thinking.
   Adult: You're just thinking?
   Adam: Yes.
   Adult: What are you thinking about?
   Adam: Thinking 'bout leaf.

As they talk more complexly about feelings, beliefs and
thoughts, toddlers start to understand that other people
are, well . . . other. I am me and you are you. Piaget said

babies didn't even realise they had toes or knew where they ended. Now the child knows other people have other feelings and thoughts. Freud marvelled at how the 'little primitive' learned so much so fast.

Bartsch and Wellman describe three different stages of the development of the theory of 'other minds'.

Before the age of 2.0, children do not say I wish and I desire or I want.

By the age of 3.0, children are much more likely to talk of thoughts.

By the age of 4.0, children are likely to talk of how other people think and feel – and they use these words properly to explain how others behave. All this contradicts Piaget who argued children stay egocentric till they are seven. The evidence is that four-year-olds begin to see things from the perspective of others. They understand other people have other minds. And other minds have other thoughts.

If other people have other minds, these other minds will have other thoughts than your mind, even a different point of view. Just as the question of when a baby has his or her first intention matters, the question of when children get the reality of other minds matters. One kind of study has become almost standard – the false belief study.

A child is shown two dolls – John and Sally. Doll John hides an object behind a sofa. Doll Sally is then taken out of the room. While she is gone, the object is hidden in a box. Doll John has watched so he knows where the object now is. Not behind the sofa but in the box, a fact that Doll Sally does not know. Logically, when she comes back, Doll Sally should believe the object is still behind the sofa.

Children under the age of three do not understand that Doll John knows something that Doll Sally does not, that the object has been moved. Doll Sally, however, does not know as she was out of the room when the object was moved. Children who are under three who are asked to say where Doll Sally will look, reply that Sally will look in the box. They cannot grasp she has no reason to look there because the last thing she saw was the object being hidden behind the sofa.

Between three and four years of age, however, a dramatic change takes place. Most children see that from Sally's point of view, the sensible thing is to look for the object where she last saw it (i.e. behind the sofa); the three-year-olds begin to 'see' into Sally's mind. It is quite logical for Sally to look behind the sofa because that was where she saw it being put. The fact it has been moved while she was out of the room doesn't matter. Her belief is logical if false; 94 per cent of four-year-olds understood the point according to one study (Joseph and Tager Flusberg, 1999).

Autism

Niko Tinbergen, who won a Nobel Prize for studies of animal behaviour, had an autistic child in his wider family which made him interested in the topic. To him, autistic children often seemed to behave like frightened animals. They sometimes took refuge, he found, in strange displacement activities which reminded him of birds standing on one leg or an ostrich burying its head in the sand. Too much eye contact scared some vulnerable children, Tinbergen told me. And like an ostrich, their answer was to act bizarrely. Which, of course, did not really help.

Nowadays, there is a better understanding of the symptoms of autism. The best seller *The Curious Incident of the Dog in the Night Time* (Haddon, 2004) gave a marvellous insight into how autistic children think and feel. Sadly there has also been a steep rise in the number of children who are affected by autism and its milder form, Asperger's syndrome. There is controversy about whether this rise is real or a case of parents reporting problems more. 'Recent work suggests autistic kids are just over stimulated; their brains are too open to too many experiences and so shut down' (Baron Cohen, 2008). That has some parallels with Tinbergen's ideas.

For parents who feel their child is not developing normally the problem is to what to look for. I have said before that being a parent can be terrifying. A friend of mine has been concerned that his child is showing signs of autism and has been trying to find proper guidance on what the symptoms are. He and his wife have met a peculiar problem. His child's school is quite eager to have the child formally diagnosed as that means the school will get more resources.

In July 2000 *The Journal of the Royal Society of Medicine* listed 18 symptoms of what are now often called 'autism spectrum disorders'. The word spectrum matters because some children with such disorders are very difficult to handle all the time while others are far more manageable. There is no comforting way of describing autism.

The signs – a less pejorative word than the too medical 'symptoms' – include problems in making good eye contact and odd body postures and gesture when dealing with other people. Children with autism don't easily develop relationships with other children and they can make weird responses when other people show feelings. They don't bring objects for other people to look at and play with, for example. Some children have compulsive routines and rituals; repetitive mannerisms – the child flaps or twists fingers or hands or performs odd body movements.

Children with autism tend to have problems with speech and some compensate by using gesture or mime. This can lead some people to try to communicate with such a child by using mime. Some children – and some parents – really object.

Finally, there is what has become a key area of research. It has been suggested that autistic children do not have the mirroring neurons most children have and that affects their abillity to play, as play involves imitation. They do not pretend play because pretending often involves anticipating what another child will do. I can't play Indian, if I have no sense of, or just don't care, what cowboy will do.

But help is available – and probably more effective help than ever before. If your child doesn't seem to respond normally to social situations, go to the GP but also get advice from the National Autistic Society which runs an Autism Helpline. It provides a general information service for those affected by what are called 'autism spectrum disorders' in the UK as well as a Parent to Parent Line run by volunteers who are themselves parents of children with autism.

My non-electrical father

I believe parents have a better chance of helping their children intelligently if they understand the particular shape of their children's minds as Kagan has suggested.

I'll be personal again. My father had a real gift for languages. He spoke French, English, Hebrew, Arabic, some German and some Turkish. He could quote long extracts from the Bible and the Koran. On the other hand, if you asked my father to fix a plug, no hope! I am sure he never handled a screwdriver in his life. He never learned to drive. One of the more comic incidents in his life was when he ran a sandwich bar in Oxford Street. He could discuss how the Earl of Sandwich had created the sandwich and quote the lines about cucumber sandwiches from Oscar Wilde's *The Importance of Being Earnest*. But make a sandwich? Don't ask the impossible of a man who could recite the Ten Commandments in seven languages.

I have inherited some of my father's lack of practical skills. While writing a book on psychological tests, I gave myself the Columbia Driving Skills Test, the best established paper and pencil test of driving aptitude. I passed with flying colours.

The only problem was that I failed my driving test at the age of 17 on every count except parroting The Highway Code. While doing lessons before my second test, I had a life changing experience. Guildford Town Hall crashed into my vehicle. The Town Hall was driving far too fast. I gave up any driving ambitions.

Many people have gaps in their brains where the synapses don't connect too well. Nearly 70 years ago in *The Normal Child*, C.W. Valentine (1942) confessed he could not remember names well. He also couldn't read Greek letters which was a shame for an educated man at that time. He reported testing children who had an IQ of about 150 (i.e. in the top 1 per cent of the population) but who could not recognise a tune. On the other hand, he had seen a perfectly average child who, at the age of two, could sing back 63 different tunes.

One of the lovely things about Valentine's book is the way you feel he has such fun with his children. The book is still charming and worthwhile. Valentine knew that to be a good father you should play with your children as much as possible. Find your inner child, your long dormant child, the child in yourself. It will make you a better father.

13

Sex and young children

So far this book has been suitable for a family audience. But the next paragraph is X rated.

'I know what oral sex is,' the girl said on the 135 bus. She was 13 I guessed and was wearing the uniform of a Catholic school in Stepney.

'Do you?' one of her friends asked, sceptically.

'Talking about sex.'

The other girls didn't laugh. They were embarrassed and became more embarrassed because they realised I could hear every word. One shook her head and motioned for her friend to come close. Then she whispered the truth. I wish I could have filmed the shock on the girl's face as she realised she did not know her arse from her elbow, so to speak.

When Freud suggested children had sexual feelings, the shock made respectable 1900 Vienna reel. Fathers and mothers need to know what psychology can tell us about children and sexuality for two reasons. It will make you a better, more sensitive parent. And it happens to be interesting.

The Oedipus Complex

Oedipus stands for all boys, Freud argued, for all men. The story is harrowing. Oedipus arrives in Thebes, a city that is being ravaged by the plague. The oracles say the plague will not stop until someone solves the famous riddle of the Sphinx. It went: What walks on four legs, then on two legs, then on three legs?

The answer is a human being. A baby crawls on all fours; an adult stands up on two legs; when we are old we need a cane and become three legs.

Oedipus solves the riddle, becomes the new king and marries Jocasta, the widow of King Laius who had been murdered.

For 12 years everyone prospers. Then the plague comes back and Jocasta's brother Creon announces the plague will disappear only if the person who murdered King Laius is exiled. Oedipus sends for the blind seer, Tiresias, to find who the killer was. As it's a myth, if the man is blind, he must see more than us; he has the inner eye.

Tiresias doesn't want to speak but Oedipus insists. Finally, Tiresias announces Oedipus himself killed Laius and so the King must be exiled. The awful truth comes out. Oedipus did kill Laius at the junction of the three roads but he thought the King was a robber. Then worse, long ago, because of a prophecy Queen Jocasta gave her baby son to a shepherd and told him to leave the mite to die up in the mountains. When he is summoned, the shepherd admits he spared the baby. Oedipus is Jocasta's son and did murder Laius, his father, at the junction of the three roads. As a result everyone ends tragically. (Well, it is a Greek tragedy.)

Jocasta hangs herself. Oedipus stabs out his eyes. Then he goes into exile. Freud felt that the myth touched a universal truth poetically. Oedipus acted out what every child wants unconsciously.

Freud found his patients resisted this truth because what it implied seemed so unbearable. He wrote: 'When I insist to one of my patients on the frequency of Oedipus dreams in which the dreamer has sexual intercourse with his own mother, he often replies "I have no recollection of having had any such dream".'

The denials did not last long. The typical patient would then dream some 'inconspicuous and indifferent dream'. When Freud analysed this, it soon turned out to be 'a dream with the same content – once more an Oedipus dream'. Denials and defences didn't work; the conscious mind screened, censored, softened, lied to itself, fiddled, faddled, fudged but it could not change the raw truths of the unconscious. 'Disguised dreams of sexual intercourse with the dreamer's mother are many times more frequent than straightforward ones', Freud claimed.

Suggesting respectable men and women fantasied about incest with their parents made many people hate psychoanalysis, Freud knew. But he had to tell the truth. In our dreams we are all father killers and seducers of mothers. The Oedipus Complex has been the subject of much controversy. Freud argued children only coped with these unconscious conflicts by suppressing their sexuality when they were about six. They then went into what he called 'latency' and became a-sexual. Latency allows boys to resolve the Oedipus Complex by identifying with their father. The wise dad knowing this spends time with his son. Son and dad do things together and bond more. If dad is a hero and dad 'has' mum, and I am like dad, I somehow have mum too. The price I have to pay is to stop being a sexual being. For now.

Where does that leave fathers and daughters? Freud wrote much less about them partly, some suspect, because he felt guilty about the fact that he analysed his youngest daughter Anna himself, an extraordinary thing to do which today would be seen as highly unethical. One analyst later said he could understand the temptation Freud felt because fathers often do want to be the central man in their daughter's lives for all of their lives.

As with boys, the trick with girls is to love and then let go. Freud was able to do this with two of his daughters but never with Anna who he considered the most gifted of all his children. He saw off the first man who wanted to marry her and no one else even stood a chance. As a father of daughters, Freud is not the best example.

Dads should get involved in all kinds of activities with their daughters. I have already discussed the different games young boys and young girls tend to play. As children become sexualised younger and younger, dads may have to deal with an eight-year-old girl who wants to go shopping and try make up. Since most men hate going shopping, think of other things you can do with your daughter – and agree with her mother that eight is the age for face paint rather than lipstick.

Some basic ideas for what to do with your daughter:

Girls increasingly like going to football.

Take your daughter to a museum or a film.

Do not nag her into doing stereotypically blokey things with you. Your ten-year-old daughter is unlikely to be interested in vintage cars but you could strike a deal. You'll go with her to see old clothes or costumes – you can't do much shopping in a museum like the Victoria and Albert – and then she'll come with you to your vintage cars.

Many girls love horse riding which can be expensive but you can as a birthday treat get riding lessons and go to see how she does.

Sex education

I have not travelled enough on Dutch buses to know whether children there also get it all wrong about oral sex. But the British government is now looking to the Dutch as well as the Scandinavian experts on sex education. Some aspects of progressive education tend to bring out the sceptic in me, I confess.

In October 2008, the British government announced we were going Dutch. Lessons about sex and relationships would become compulsory in English schools. Five-year-olds would learn basic biology. The government Minister for Schools, Jim Knight said in perfect PC speak: 'We are not suggesting that five and six-year-olds should be taught sex. What we are saying is we need to improve in particular the relationship education, improve the moral framework and moral understanding around which we then talk about sex later on in a child's education.'

Simon Blake of the sexual health charity 'Brook' could not contain himself with joy. That sex was to become part of the national curriculum was 'absolutely brilliant'. Children could become comfortable with the facts of life. Not everyone was so enthused, however. A poll of parents showed many thought five-year-olds had better things to do; 64 per cent of parents believed sex education should not start until children were at least 11 years old. Just over a third (36 per cent) said they did not think children should learn about contraception until they were 13. No one dared ask the burning issue on the 135 bus.

At what age should oral sex be on the syllabus?

The Department of Schools imagines a splendid syllabus; children will also learn about relationship skills, rights and responsibilities, contraception, pregnancy and sexually transmitted infections and risky behaviours. British children will become more mature, more like the Dutch and Swedish children. There would be fewer teenage pregnancies, an issue that concerns the government. The concern makes sense as there seems to be a strong link between teenage pregnancy and mental health problems. One survey showed that a quarter of teenage parents had a probable psychiatric disorder. A study of young women with conduct disorders showed that a third became pregnant before the age of 17.

A recent study by The Trust for the Study of Adolescence covered this issue and gathered some good case histories. Bethany Cole, a 16-year-old schoolgirl from Buckingham, wanted schools to have more sex education.

Most people I know haven't had sex yet and didn't have sex before turning 16. They don't care about breaking the law as they think no one will find out. Some male friends joke about sex and say that they've 'had it', but I suspect much of that is just male bravado. Me and my girlfriends do talk about sex; for example, if someone has had sex for the first time with a new boyfriend, or asks us if she can catch a sexually transmitted infection from something she did at the weekend. But my friends are pretty responsible, and use condoms, for example.

Proper sex education would make for fewer teenage pregnancies and fewer sexually transmitted infections.

It seems as important for children to know about sex for their own safety given our concerns about child abuse.

Child abuse

Some psychologists like Carl Rogers, the founder of humanist therapy, were aware of child sexual abuse in the 1930s and tried to get doctors and social workers to realise it happened. But he did not succeed that much. In 1975 as a young social worker, Julia Ross was astonished when a 15-year-old client told her she hated the fact that her father kept touching her breast. We let ourselves be blind for a long time partly because abuse is shocking and partly because experts have often had little sense about how to question children.

In 1980 Stephen Ceci, the psychologist who taught his daughter to lie with mixed success, received an unexpected phone call. A judge he knew called for advice.

The judge was trying a case where a woman's body had been found concreted below her living room. Her husband had killed her, her sisters said, but the main witness was the dead woman's son. The police said the boy remembered seeing his father hit his mother with a baseball bat. But the boy was just four years old when he had seen this.

The judge asked Ceci: 'if he could believe a child's memories of such an event?'

Ceci told me that his work on childhood memory had concentrated on how children recall lists on nonsense syllables such as CIC, TOB and GUB. 'I was clueless,' he admitted. He had never studied how children remember real life events but he realised how important the subject was.

Children have surprisingly good memories, he found, but the way adults ask questions rarely helps.

'After ten years, I'm struck by how well children, as young as three, remember ordinary events,' Ceci told me; 95 per cent of children can describe an event which happened three months earlier quite accurately. 'The problem is the adults,' Ceci said because adults phrase questions in ways that baffle, confuse and upset children. That is especially true when the subject is abuse.

Young children hate talking about embarrassing events – and can easily lapse into awkward silences. These silences provoke anxiety in professionals such as social workers, police, lawyers, psychologists. If they think a child is being abused, if they don't get answers, if they feel the child is stalling, they feel under pressure. They bombard the child with more questions; then the child feels under pressure. In such a situation professionals often start to suggest answers and the child agrees.

The right way, Ceci learned, is for interviewers to be patient, to wait and to prompt the child gently and objectively. But the 'good' police and social workers want to protect the child so they often ask leading questions which muddy the waters. Well-meaning officers word them in ways that don't just influence what children say but also what children start to believe. 'Suggestive' questions can make a child create 'false beliefs' in his or her own mind.

Ceci tested his ideas in a classroom. Children aged three, four and six years had an unexpected visitor, Sam Stone. Sam walked in, said something about the book being read to the class, and then walked out after perhaps two minutes. Children remembered Sam coming into the room and said, accurately, that nothing else of any interest had taken place.

'But if you start to seed things,' Ceci said, 'you can make children believe something very different happened.' Some children were told Sam was clumsy and often broke things; others got leading questions which implied there had been trouble when Sam was in class. This seeding changed what children remembered; 72 per cent of them embroidered the story (i.e. the truth) and many added details of how destructive Sam had been. But that was all down to suggestion. In fact, Sam hadn't banged desks or ripped up books.

Question children in a way that 'seeds' doubts and they easily start to believe events that did not happen did happen; 35 per cent of six-year-olds can develop such false beliefs. Younger children are even more susceptible.

Ceci showed me a dramatic video. A five-year-old boy was asked about an incident in his basement of his home. The interviewer spoke about a mouse in the basement though there had never been any such mouse. Then, the interviewer asked how the boy's finger got caught in the mousetrap and how the boy felt when he was taken to hospital. It was total make believe. But, after a few weeks of such insidious questioning, Ceci's five-year-old had come to believe there had been a mouse and that he had got his finger caught in the mousetrap.

The boy 'confessed' he had been taken to the hospital because his finger hurt so much. This rather fairy-tale study shows how easy it is for well-meaning social workers and police officers to prompt children so they start to remember incidents which never happened. When dealing with allegations of abuse, the consequences can be tragic.

Some of the confusions Ceci described were almost farcical. A woman rang the police when her three-year-old daughter said 'daddy put his pee-pee in my pee-pee'. It seemed evidence of abuse, but the truth was to do with flushing the toilet. The girl had peed and not flushed; her father had gone to the bathroom later, peed and so put his pee-pee into her pee-pee.

Ceci's work offers lessons. If parents, police or social workers get too anxious about getting a result, they will confuse – and quite possibly distress – the child. Given our concerns about problems with child protection, his work needs to be known outside academic circles.

Excuses

Those who study and try to work with abusers find that they often justify it by saying the children really wanted the experience or were curious about sex. This is pernicious nonsense.

If you find yourself even thinking of touching your children inappropriately or getting them to touch you inappropriately don't fool yourself. Go and get help. Never delude yourself that a child really wants sexual attention from you.

14

The arts and smarts of discipline

"Spanking or non-spanking section?"

For 2,500 years philosophers, teachers and priests have tried to work out how best to socialise and discipline children. When I first went to school in London, we were not just caned – a formal and terrifying ritual – but informally beaten with a wooden tennis racket. The Latin master liked doing it. You got beaten if you were bad at Latin to motivate you and you got beaten if you were really good at Latin – to teach you humility.

Today the question of how best to discipline children worries parents, police and experts because it often feels as if youth is out of control. Scotland Yard say that 171 gangs of under 18s operate in London. Television reflects our uncertainties. There are nearly as many shows on how to cope with children as on gardening and some of these Psycho Nanny Knows Best shows have become big hits. It is a measure of our failure to learn how to discipline children that in the West there are many agonised debates about why our children behave so badly. Sociologists point to the breakdown of parental authority, the death of deference, sex, drugs and rock 'n' roll, not to mention the ozone layer.

Psychologists have known since the 1930s that certain kinds of punishments don't work – and yet we still use them. We cling to what does not work out of ignorance, anxiety and exasperation. The press doesn't help as it tends to demonize 'bad' children. The truth is that psychology has failed to get its message over as well as it should.

In many families traditionally the dad was mainly responsible for discipline. Discipline till very recently has included getting beaten. My father certainly did that to me. And I was frightened of him and hated it.

Self Analysis 9
Ask yourself:
Are you apt to get very angry when your children misbehave?
Do you think children often do it just to annoy their parents?
Did your mum or your dad smack you often?

Twenty years ago, Graziano (Graziano and Namaste, 1990) studied 679 college freshmen and found that 93.2 per cent of them had been spanked as children. They had accepted this as normal; most of them said they intended to carry on the tradition and spank their own children. Only the 6.8 per cent who were not spanked as children did not accept it was a good idea. The freshmen of 1990 are today's parents.

Amaze-ing rats

The behaviourists were the first psychologists to offer scientific programmes of discipline. Behaviourism claimed we are all conditioned by the way we are punished and rewarded. The two most influential behaviourists, John B. Watson (1878–1958) and B.F. Skinner (1904–1990), were both committed to using psychology to help parents bring up children as well as possible.

Skinner claimed you could shape the behaviour of children and of criminals just the way you could shape the behaviour of rats and pigeons – by subtle rewards. If a rat started to run down a maze, Skinner gave it a pellet of food and continued to dole out rewards till the rat had learned its way round the whole maze. After that, the most effective rewards were intermittent. A rat who had been trained to press a lever would get a reward of sugar, say 5 times in 100. The intermittently rewarded rat learned to keep on pressing. Using this pattern of reinforcement, Skinner taught pigeons to play ping-pong and to guide missiles. The Pentagon refused to use the pigeons to bomb Russia with missiles because that would be cruel to animals!

Skinner applied his ideas in institutions like prisons and children's homes and claimed success as long as there were what he termed 'token' economies; in a token economy, you get fixed rewards for good behaviour. You get 3 points if you make your bed in the morning and 5 points if you help make lunch. Points are like Airmiles. They buy privileges like being allowed out of an evening. Bad behaviour costs points. Hitting someone would lose you 10 points.

In a token-economy system, however, you are never punished physically or ridiculed.

The most effective way to bring up a child, Skinner argued, is to select the desirable behaviours and reward them with praise, points and attention. Rewards worked better than punishments. Skinner even wrote a novel, *Walden Two*, about a community which lived by these rules.

I interviewed Skinner twice in the 1970s and I did not find a happy shaper. He was angry at what he saw as malicious attempts to paint him as a punishment-crazed control freak. He was puzzled people did not want to hear what he was saying. It was hardly demonic. Don't punish kids for doing wrong, reward them for doing right.

A hostile press even accused him and his wife of bringing up their daughter in a Skinner box, part cot, part cage; she was imprisoned and punished if she broke the rules. That was a total lie, he told me. When Stanley Kubrick's *A Clockwork Orange* was released, Skinner was livid critics claimed the punishments used on the young thug/hero were ones he recommended. Electrodes were implanted in the hero's brain and the thug only had to think an antisocial thought and his brain was zapped. Skinner condemned this as a torture, but that did not stop the press claiming it was all his theory.

Skinner and John B. Watson, in fact, argued that 'spare the rod and spoil the child' was not merely cruel, but also not very effective. They argued that physical punishment rarely works and can cause serious neurotic side effects. It was more sensible to get a child to behave well by rewarding them for positive behaviour. If one wanted to punish, the 'best' – and safest – punishment was to withhold attention and affection.

Watson, in particular, said one should tell a child why he or she had done wrong. He believed that the family should sit together to discuss problems. His son James told me they did do so though his father took to drink when his wife Rosalie died.

Social conditions are very different now from the 1930s. Children today question their parents in ways that would once have been unthinkable. Deference is dying; no one believes in authority; everything can be questioned by everybody. But that does not mean the behaviourists were wrong.

Authoritarian discipline

Baumrind (1988) argued there were authoritarian, authoritative, emotionally controlling and permissive parents –
four different types. The research made it clear that authoritative parenting was the best style but it is useful to
analyse all four.

The authoritarian father believes in strong discipline,
clear rules, no arguments and the right to smack a dis-
obedient child. Parents who practise strong discipline often
care about their children a great deal, but tend to see them
as being unable to listen to reason. Children have to be
trained like animals.

Authoritative

Baumrind clearly believed this was the best style. Authoritative parents are warm, loving, responsive and supportive
but that does not mean that they don't set boundaries.
In his moving book about the Soham tragedy, *Goodbye
Dearest Holly*, Kevin Wells who was devoted to his daughter
explained that they became anxious when Holly was 45
minutes late coming home because they had laid down rules
about being home on time and explained why that mattered.
When she was late it had to be that something was badly
wrong.

Authoritative parents respect their child's indepen-
dence, their point of view and their personality. They talk
to their children. When they stop the children doing something, they don't just issue an edict but explain why. They
demand mature behaviour, but mature behaviour does not
always mean doing the conventional thing.

Being authoritative does not mean showing no feelings.
Zahn Waxler *et al.* (1979) found that where mothers
explained, it left a lasting impact. Typically mothers said
things like, 'Look what you did. Don't you see you hurt
Amy?' This worked much better than either hitting their
child or just telling her to stop. This style is, of course,
the very opposite of indifference. The parent shows he, or

she, cares because he or she is emotional, emotional but controlled enough to explain what a child has done wrong immediately.

Emotional control

Parents who believe in this approach will smack a child, but only as a very last resort. Children will learn if you praise them when they are good and tell them off when they are bad. The key phrase is 'tell them off'; that includes emotional withdrawal and, very often, making the child feel bad about himself or herself because they have let their parents down. But the emotional disciplinarian has to be really pushed to punish a child physically.

Permissive

Such parents trust in the spirit of the child. They believe that if parents try to impose their will on the child, it is a kind of emotional abuse. Permissive mothers and fathers ignore boundaries, trust (probably too much) in the child, especially the young child and set very few rules. Smacking a child is out of the question.

Baumrind looked at the effects of the four different styles. She compared children before they went to school and when they were nine years old. She asked teachers to rate their behaviour. Children who had been brought up authoritatively were more competent intellectually and socially; they were also more friendly and co-operative than the children of authoritarian or permissive parents.

These results are what Watson and Skinner would have predicted. Harsh parenting makes children more aggressive in the long run but we still have problems in accepting that. We need to ask why.

In 1990, two years after Baumrind published her research, The European Court of Human Rights ruled in the case in which a nine-year-old had been beaten by his stepfather. The Court did not go so far as to judge corporal punishment violated Article 3 of the Convention on the

Rights of the Child. But it did rule that children must not have their personal integrity violated as they are vulnerable. The stepfather had breached Article 3.

The ruling in the case of A v UK has been influential – and inspired research. Studies in Scotland in 2002 showed toddlers and pre-school children were the most likely to be smacked. Parents admitted they hit children usually in moments of particularly high stress and that afterwards they felt guilty. Nearly everyone agreed that it was better to bring up children using non-physical methods of discipline such as taking away a treat (NFO System Three for Scottish Executive, 2002).

Scotland changed its laws in 2003 and made it illegal to punish children by shaking, hitting on the head, using a belt, cane, slipper, wooden spoon or other implement. The law did not ban smacking altogether but warned it could be dangerous. It is easy to forget how frail children are when you are angry. What feels like a light slap to an adult can hurt and frighten a small child. Resorting to violence also sets a bad example. Smacking teaches children to hit out at people who are doing things they don't like.

The leading journal *Child Development* carried results of surveys from seven different countries in the November/ December 2005 issue. It aimed to settle controversies about punishment. Unfortunately it only used a small sample, only 336 families in all the seven countries, but the results do nothing to support smacking.

Psychologists from the United States, Italy, Hong Kong, Sweden, India, Thailand and Kenya asked mothers how often they smacked or beat their children, how often they thought other parents in their country used physical discipline and whether their children were anxious, got into fights or bullied others.

Mothers in Thailand were the 'softest', least likely to smack; mothers in Kenya were the 'hardest'. Culture had an influence. In countries where it was acceptable to beat children, mothers beat them more and not just when the children were aggressive or anxious. In these countries children who were smacked were less aggressive and less anxious than children from countries where smacking was rare. But in Europe and America where smacking is now considered too harsh, it seems not to make children either more obedient or less anxious.

A later study shows how complex issues can become. Michael Sheehan and Malcolm Watson (2008) followed 440 children and their mothers for five years. The children were aged 10 on average when the study started. Ideally psychologists would have been filming the family secretly to judge, first, how mothers did discipline the children and, second, what the children were doing to provoke them, if they were doing much at all. Instead, mothers answered questions about their style of parenting and their children's behaviour. Imperfect as its methods were, the research showed parenting 'style' affects children's behaviour and also that the children's behaviour influences their mothers. If children were aggressive when they were small, their mothers disciplined them more and in a more combative way. They yelled at them and smacked them. But even these mothers did not just smack; they also tried to reason. Still, Sheehan and Watson concluded that 'a greater use of harsh, aggressive discipline by mothers predicted increased future aggressive behaviour by their children'.

A good summary of American traditions is to be found in Murray A. Straus and Denise A. Donnelly's (2004) *Beating the Devil Out of Them: Corporal Punishment in American Families and Its Effects on Children*. They argue spanking has no measurable beneficial effects at all, and that it is associated with many long term negative effects. The more children are spanked, the more they assault their brothers, sisters and other children and the more antisocial behaviour they display. Spanked children, as they get older, show higher levels of alcoholism, depression, masochistic fantasy, criminal activity and suicidal ideas.

Parents who spank their children are also more likely to physically abuse them and 'spanking' parents are more likely to physically abuse each other. The evidence against spanking is like the evidence against smoking. We have to stop fooling ourselves. Smoking kills and spanking damages. Both are 'addictive practices' and smokers and spankers justify their 'sins' the same way. *'I've smoked for forty*

years and I feel fine!' 'I was spanked and it never did ME
any harm!'

Delusions both!

I am against smacking in almost any situation. But if
you are pushed to smack your child there are some funda-
mental rules. First, babies should never be smacked.
Second, with any child you have to:

1 Stay in control.
2 Smacking and spanking should never turn into an
   assault, and repeated hitting of a child is an assault.
3 Explain to your child why you are about to spank or
   smack him or her. You can't hope to do that when your
   child is too young to understand what you are saying.

The only remotely acceptable reason to smack or spank is to
make a very serious point very forcefully when a child has
done something wrong or dangerous. Never do it to release
your frustrations.

What follows is one of my more shameful memories but
not because I hit either of my boys.

The good Quaker girl and bullying

Bullying is not just obvious – hitting an unpopular child in
the playground – but insidious – teasing, playing nasty
practical jokes or deliberately leaving someone out of
things. Often children who are being bullied are ashamed
as well as frightened, and keep quiet about it. I know from
personal experience that this happens.

When our boys were ten and six, Aileen and I hired a
respectable seeming young woman to look after them when
they got home from school. Annabel (not her real name)
was the daughter of a couple from the local Quaker meet-
ing. That seemed a guarantee that she was responsible and
kind. We did not notice that our younger son was getting
withdrawn.

After some months, Nicholas plucked up the courage to
tell us the 'babysitter' was spiteful and sometimes violent

to our younger son. She screamed at him and, sometimes, even hit him. We had no idea. As we were very self absorbed at the time, we did not talk to the children enough about what was happening. When we found out, we sacked her at once but it had been going on for too long. If you do use a nanny or a childminder, get serious references and be very vigilant. We had totally failed to learn how to give our children the chance to explain what was wrong.

For parents the lessons are clear. Talk to other parents who used the nanny, babysitter or childminder before you take her on.

If they are being bullied, children tend to change and also tend to deny it. That is what you need to be alert for. Be ready for a bit of battle. Dads need to know that the bullied child often feels they have no control over their life.

The NSPCC have recruited the boxer, Amir Khan, to campaign against bullying. He says on their website: 'If you are being bullied don't hide it because when you hide it then there's nothing going to be solved. If you're just going to hide it it's always going to get worse and we just want to put a stop to that. And I just want to send a message across to people that if you are being bullied not to be scared.' Khan's message makes it very clear. Do not feel ashamed because you or your child is being bullied.

The advice the NSPCC website gives is good advice for dads to give their children too.

- Think up some replies to comments that the bullies are making.
- Stay in a group – child bullying is less likely to happen if bullies know you are not on your own.
- Try and find out why you are being bullied, and work out if there is anything you could do differently to stop it happening.
- It's important to find someone to talk to – they can help you think about what to do next.
- Walk away – don't worry if others think you're running away; it's more difficult for a bully to pick on someone who won't stand still!

No magic formula

For the last 60 years, psychologists have known the most effective ways of teaching discipline to most children but there are still thousands of children who live in terror of their parents. Don't do that to your kids. Be prepared to listen. Don't jump to conclusions. Give your child time. If you think your child has done something wrong, ask open-ended questions such as, 'Why did you do that?' rather than 'Did you or did you not steal Willy's truck?'. If your child does not reply quickly don't panic or harass him. These techniques may be especially relevant in stepfamilies where the dynamics may be very complex. Remember the evidence which is pretty solid.

Physical punishments are not effective.

That does not mean you cannot lay down strict rules.

You should be willing to explain why something is wrong.

The ghosts in all of us

I'm not about to go paranormal, but most of us are also influenced by invisible presences – mainly our own parents, their attitudes to discipline and how we reacted, conscious and unconscious stuff.

I have suggested there is sound evidence for Watson and Skinner's ideas. Praise, explain, discuss, punish by disapproving rather than smacking. Regrettably, not all parents will find these attitudes congenial. For some, these 'liberal' ideas will go directly against the grain of their personality. You have to draw the line if you want them to grow up decent. But the line is not a stick to beat your children with. It is also a question of how you cope with your own feelings, particularly if they seem to be getting the better of you and you are not in emotional control.

Being a good enough father requires a certain degree of honest introspection.

Self Analysis 10
Here are some situations to think about
1 *You discover your child has not gone to school and has been lying about it. Do you discuss with him why he or*

she is bunking off? Do you discuss with the mother what to do? Do you smack him the moment he comes home?

2 *Do you worry because you seem to be losing your temper a great deal?*

3 *Do you feel better after you have smacked your child? Do you feel that the problem has been sorted then?*

I want to end this chapter by offering some basic advice on how to manage anger because some fathers can sometimes be overwhelmed by it – and may be blind to the fact that fear can fuel it. No one will get their temper under control if they don't recognise what is happening to them when they feel tense and a rush of adrenaline. We talk of a rush of blood to the head but it's the adrenaline kicking in, and nature gave us adrenaline so that we could flee predators in Neanderthal times.

Anger management

Many factors affect our moods. Work, financial stress, unhappiness at home, anxiety, and we end up stressed out. As I write in 2009, the world faces, according to Ed Balls, the British Secretary of State for Children and Education, the worst recession for 100 years. To cope we turn so easily to things that don't help us cope, drink, denial, lashing out at those closest to us. As a father you can't just live for your children, but you do need to know your own moods and be willing to seek help if they are out of control.

It is useful to isolate exactly what triggers anger and, at worst, the desire to lash at your child. Some fathers have reported the following triggers:

- the baby crying
- whining
- throwing food or objects and making a mess
- demands for food
- demands for attention
- the mother fussing over the child

- the mother criticising the father
- despair and frustration the child will never stop crying, feeling that if you hit the child then it will stop.

A baby, or a toddler, is helpless, defenceless and cannot threaten you. You are not thinking or seeing straight if you are getting into a power struggle with a creature who weighs less than one or two stones. Violent men need professional counselling, but the following techniques can be useful to help you get perspective and control if you feel tempted to get violent.

Some fathers report it helps to do some relaxation and deep-breathing training. When their child screams, they learn not to get agitated, control themselves and the urge to do something violent to make themselves feel better. They breathe, they relax, they try to assess the situation and work out why the child is crying.

That pause gives them time to breathe, time to think, time to stop doing something they will regret.

Drinking demons

Alcohol always makes problems worse; studies in Britain and Australia show 80 per cent of the cases of domestic violence involve drink. A drunken father is a dangerous father (Elliott, 1995).

Many men dislike the idea of going to counselling. Instead they promise never to do it again and to control their temper. That can happen, but it is rare. To admit you need help makes one feel helpless and many men hate that. I am sorry to sound like some melodrama but the brave, the manly thing to do is to:

Admit you need help.
The admission is the first hard part.
The second hard part is to go and get it.

Abraham and his daughter

Abraham broke his daughter's arm when she was in her teens. He is a professional man and had been violent to his

wife and children for a long time. He said he did not know
what made him lose his temper. For years, he refused to
seek help; when his wife said he needed therapy, it made
him furious. Yet again the bitch thought she knew best, he
thought. Their neighbours had no idea what was going on.

One night Abraham hit his daughter very badly. He
agreed to seek counselling but it had a surprising result.
Abraham came out of it feeling that he knew why he hit
his wife and children. His wife who was better educated
than he was kept winding him up just as his mother had
done. Before going into counselling, Abraham was always
very ashamed after he lost his temper. Now, he could
explain his lack of control.

Some months later, Abraham lost it again and broke
his daughter's arm. She said she would not speak to him
again till he tried to sort it out properly. She had the courage to draw the line. This time Abraham found a counsellor
who gave him alternative ways of coping. And made one
thing crystal clear. Violence was unacceptable. Totally.

Abraham left home for a time. The crunch only came
when he felt he would lose everything if he did not change.
Under that kind of pressure, counselling finally did work.
He and his family are reunited now and he is a proud
grandfather. 'He finds his grandchildren easier than he did
his children,' his wife said.

I pointed out earlier that studies of child abuse claim a
third of adults who abuse children were themselves abused.
It is very hard to get abusers to talk honestly about what
drives them to it. Some survivors feel they have every right
to lord brute physical power over their children.

If you are violent to your child or are tempted to be
more than just once or twice when severely stressed, you
need to consider getting help. You have to face up to the
problem. If you don't, your family will be hurt psychologically as well as physically. The good news is that there is
much evidence that men can learn to manage their anger.
It is easier than getting off drugs or antidepressants.

All parents feel they fail sometimes, when it comes to
discipline. Do not beat your child and do not beat yourself
up over that. You cannot be the perfect disciplinarian any

more than you can be the perfect father. But the good enough disciplinarian lays down boundaries, does not lose his cool and is ready to explain why something is wrong.

Perhaps the only rule is to never to say 'just do as I say'. Well, not never – but as rarely as you can.

15

School

It is utterly normal for fathers to want their children to shine. But remember that history is full of successful men and women who developed late. Winston Churchill hated school, was thought something of an idiot and yet he did more to save the world than anyone else. Princess Diana did not exactly shine at school but she became an effective campaigner for causes like justice for those who have HIV and for a ban on landmines.

History is littered with parents who tried to turn their little darling into a genius and turned him or her into casualties instead. Judy Garland made her stage debut at the age of two because her mother had failed to become an actress and was determined to make her daughter a star. Even Mozart reacted against the pressure of his pushy father. If you failed to become a leading lawyer, actor, politician, industrialist, or tycoon – don't expect your kids to do it for you.

Fathers need to strike a delicate balance. The dad who will look over homework when it is finished, the dad who will discuss what music he liked when he was young, and the dad who will talk about the news on television is helping. The dad who wants to know why you didn't come first, you lazy sod, will not help his children. There is a balance. Encourage, support but don't push.

Support means listening. One good routine for fathers is to ask what happened at school from the first day a child attends. Sometimes, children won't want to talk. But if it is what you do when they start, it will become just part of the end of every day.

Always ask your child what they are doing at school. Sometimes, they will brush you off. But persevere.

If he, or she, asks you to look at homework, do it and talk about what they got right, and what they got wrong.

If he, or she, asks you to do the homework, explain why there is no point in homework if you do it for them. Add that you are happy to look at the homework when it is done, and then to talk about it. There are revision books and internet sites which allow parents to brush up their probably dim memories of what they learned in school. That can help you help your child.

British families also face a curious cultural problem in dealing with education.

How to be a clever salami

The Hungarian humorist, Georges Mikes, in *How to Be an Alien* noted Britain is the only country where you can be criticised for being too intelligent. Hungary is famous for its salamis, hence the heading. Mikes could never remember a Frenchman, a German or a Hungarian being sniped at for being 'too clever by half'. Yet, that's a perfect British barb. Bloggs is not sound, he's too clever by half. Swots were distrusted in public schools. The admired adolescent shone at cricket and passed exams without trying too hard. At Oxford till the 1970s, it was respectable to get a gentlemen's degree, a fourth. A third was sad, but a fourth showed you had not even bothered to try. Cool! Gentlemen just were – without trying.

Attitudes are changing but slowly. Does this distrust of intellect have no connection with the fact Britain still has the worst literacy record in Europe? In most European countries, a minister of education who struggled to answer a question like – what is 9×12? – would probably have been forced to resign. But not in the UK. When the then Secretary of State for Education, David Blunkett took 13 seconds – by which time an Olympic sprinter would have run 140 metres – to work out what 9×12 was, no one suggested he should stand outside the House of Commons wearing a dunce's cap.

In the last 20 years, parents have been encouraged to get more involved with schools. Parent governors help run schools and that means dads have to go back to school more than before. Always go to parent–teacher evenings. Your child will want you to turn up looking good so that the next day class mates don't say my dad said your dad's a scruff.

Parent–teacher relations

Remember parent–teacher evenings are held for the convenience of the school. If there isn't enough time to discuss something that is worrying you, don't make a fuss but make an appointment so you can go back when the teacher has time.

While it's important to encourage and support your child, be realistic. Do not expect your child to come top in everything or blame the school if she or he does not.

In Britain, roughly 22,000 children bunk off school every day for no good reason. I did it myself in the 1960s as I explained, to avoid parading up and down in the Cadet Corps.

If you discover your child is playing truant, don't go ballistic. You need to stay calm and talk to your child to find out why. Is it laziness? Is it that they are scared? Talking is, as ever, vital. Ask what is making them do it. Is it that they hate school? Is it that they hate a particular teacher? There are solutions. You could ask the school to put your child in a different class. You could even consider changing schools.

Do not turn a blind eye. Truancy can often lead to even more serious problems. Official statistics show that around one pupil in every 1,000 is permanently excluded from school every year in the UK.

There is a list of books at the end worth consulting to help your children in both primary and secondary school. From a psychological point of view, don't panic. If your child is struggling at school, keep calm about it. Discuss it with your partner, your child and the teachers. Don't be upset if they suggest your child should be assessed by an educational psychologist. They sometimes can be very practical. There are also organisations which offer advice on how to get help with school problems.

Zen and the art of passing exams

Children are tested from the start of school. Some will enjoy that but most kids don't. The following principles apply from seven or eight years of age. Think of yourself as a trainer. You need to create, without putting intense pressure on, an atmosphere in which your child can prepare for and feel confident about the ordeal to come. Make sure your child can find peace and quiet to do homework and, when they are older, a comfortable place to revise.

Much of this is common sense. Children often get anxious and confused. Make sure they know what they will be tested on and that they have the pens, pencils, and rubbers they will need. If a test is freaking out a child, talk to the school about it.

In almost every country in the world teenagers take exams. As they prepare, good enough parents have to coax and cope, bring cups of tea and cake, say they have been there and that it will be all right on the day. The exam is an ordeal. By pen and calculator.

Some simple tips. Make sure children start revision in plenty of time. Talk with them to plan a revision timetable that's realistic, flexible, and linked to what they will be tested on.

There's no 'right' way to revise and things will have changed since you sat exams so don't insist your child does it like you did. But it is useful to suggest your child practise timed exam questions and papers. They will get a good idea of what the real exam will be like.

If your child is stressed, you can discuss the following with them and practise it together. There are similarities to the routine I discussed if you find you are getting very angry.

Relaxation routine for dad and child

- Close your eyes and breathe slowly and deeply.
- Locate any areas of tension and try to relax those muscles; imagine the tension disappearing.

- Relax each part of the body, from your feet to the top of your head.
- As you focus on each part of your body, think of warmth, heaviness and relaxation.
- After 20 minutes, take some deep breaths and stretch.

If you live in a Buddhist culture this Zen breathing should come naturally.

Zen won't help with many other mistakes. One very common one is not to read each question correctly. Instead of answering *Why was Henry VIII so keen on the dissolution of the monasteries?* students answer *Why was Henry VIII so keen on dissipation?* Amuse yourself and your children by making up silly questions to emphasise the need to read the real question in the exam properly, understand it and, then, answer it in full.

After the exam is over, give your child the chance to talk about how they answered but don't wallow in post-mortem blues. That will only stress them if they feel they have not done as well as they could.

Be realistic, and help your child be realistic. We are all different. Remember what research on IQ showed. Exam success isn't everything. If your child does end up doing badly, it won't be the end of the world. Facing up to the worst will enable them to think about what they could do next. There may well be another chance to take the exam, or an altogether different path may open up.

Always remember that your child is learning for herself or himself, not to make up for what you see as your failures. At the end of the book I discuss the miseries that can happen if a father wants to turn a child into a replica, the great success you feel you have not become.

16

Modern stepfamily life

The Old English word 'steop-' means 'bereave'. And that catches an important fact. Every stepfamily has had to face trauma – death or divorce, the great losses of life so you can hardly expect it to be easy to live in one. In the past there was also stigma. Marriage was forever, divorce a disgrace and if your father died, it was bound to be your fault somehow.

Today, stepfamilies are one more part of our multi-cultural multi-sexual social weave. Well, that is the theory. One in three American families is in a stepfamily and 1,300 new stepfamilies are formed there each day. *Stepfamily*, the national organisation, estimate there are between 2.5 and 3 million stepfamilies in the UK. Stepmum and stepdad are no longer exotic, but that does not make it easy for stepkid. Some research suggests that 50 per cent of stepchildren hate their stepfathers.

Stepfamily stress is no 'postmodern' fancy. So many myths and fairy tales tell of wicked stepmothers and stepfathers. Then, there is true history. In 1831, ten-year-old Charles Baudelaire was introduced by his mother to his new 'father', General Aupick. Baudelaire's father was dead, his mother had fallen in love but she had not told her son. Not till just before her wedding. Some biographers see Aupick as honourable but misguided; others give him the traditional role of the stepmonster. The General took his new stepson to the Pyrenées which led to Baudelaire's first published poem, *Incompatibility*. The trip was terrible; the poem wasn't. But the angry General sent the boy on a character-building trip to India. Baudelaire locked himself in his cabin in protest – he was good at protest – and accused the General of poisoning his relationship with his mother and of cheating him out of his inheritance of 75,000 francs.

General Aupick was lucky to live in the past. Today Baudelaire would have hired a lawyer and sued the medals and pants off him. The problem with the Baudelaires was that they did not re-blend. Sigmund Freud's family, however, did. He had two half brothers from his father's first marriage and was very fond of one of them, at least. The Freuds did 'blend' or 'reconstitute' their families – foodie metaphors gone mad.

Some experts complain this label suggests members of a stepfamily blend into a new family unit and abandon their loyalty to other outside family members. The word 'blend' leads to unrealistic expectations when stepfamily life is often confusion, conflict and pain for children, mothers and fathers. And let's be clear about the jargon. To be blended, fruit, veg and other raw foods have to go through the blender which beats, shreds and shakes their stuff before turning out something smooth and tasty.

In the postmodern metrosexual blender, stepdad may be living with a new partner and her children, but only seeing his own biological children part-time because they live with their mother. At bedtime, he knows her new bloke is helping put his kids to bed while he is putting some other man's kids to bed. That's not easy.

Under the same roof, we can find the following:

biological father/biological child; stepfather/stepchild;

biological mother/biological child; stepmother/stepchild; brother/sister; stepbrother/stepsister.

It takes sophisticated social and emotional skills to deal with such a mix of relationships, especially when many of those involved will have been damaged. The children are likely to feel they have been abandoned by their true father and will miss him. The conflicts can be traumatic, comical and, of course, comical-traumatic.

Don't try to drink your way out of trouble. Dads, don't go on a bender because you're in the blender!

My own experiences as a stepfather led me to make a comedy, *Dead Cool*, about the rows between a teenage boy and his mother's new squeeze. The boy hates his potential stepfather and can't bear the thought of his mother making love with him – in my hero's mind they make so much noise Canary Wharf rattles. The boy hits on an inspired strategy to make his stepdad suffer. The boy makes friends with his stepdad's ex-wife. But fact is sadder than fiction.

Stepfamily blues

Some of the most solid research on stepfamilies is still that by Gill Gorell Barnes. She reported a study of 444 children born in 1958, 50 of whom were brought up in stepfamilies (Gorell Barnes *et al.*, 1998). The children often were confused. When a parent left, sometimes, they did not know what had happened to their real mother or father, or when, or if, they would ever see them again. One child said her mum just introduced 'us to this new man one day and that he was going to be living with us'. Adults made the rules. Ace emotional intelligence there.

Mothers were better than fathers at preparing children for a new relationship, but even they were often secretive. Children do not like seeing their parents as sexual beings and parents know that. Some of Gorell Barnes' subjects said they hated seeing their mother and the new stepfather being physically affectionate. Parents know this and don't want to upset their children. To spare pain and embarrassment, nobody tells the children about the new man or the new woman till they absolutely have to.

The stepfather was not generally expected to do much. The children did not usually call him dad and many saw him 'more as an uncle'; he got involved but not that involved. He might cast a quick eye over homework or take the family for a spin in the car as a treat. But he wasn't like a real dad.

Many stepchildren said they hated the new stepfather, Gorell Barnes and her colleagues found, but their mother was less tense and happier than before. Children as young as eight could see that. The bloke was not much but mum was happier. And some children escaped as soon as they could.

Many of Gorell Barnes' sample left home early and married early. They wanted emotional stability, but did not usually find it, as they tended to get divorced more than average. A cycle of unhappiness set in. Today there is less stigma about stepfamilies because they are more common but research shows that living in one is getting harder if anything.

Acting Out

One of the most moving descriptions of mental health problems as a teenager is Matthew Huggins *I'll Love You If* (2009). Huggins' mother was 16 years old when he was born and soon had two other children. It was hard for her to cope and her eldest child got little of the love and attention he needed. Huggins' father was not around much.

By the age of six Huggins showed signs of depression. When his mother moved a new man in, the depression – and frustration – got worse. At the age of eleven, Huggins set fire to the living room and ended up running away to Southend. He thought his real father lived there. In Southend Huggins climbed on to the pier and threatened to throw himself off. The police talked him down. Within weeks Huggins was in care.

In care, in two children's homes and a therapeutic community, Huggins was bullied and abused. He also spent time in emergency foster placements. In one the foster mother insisted he take medication; that would solve all his problems and, then, bizarrely she would take him to New York for a holiday. Huggins resisted the medication and ended up running away. The therapeutic community helped more than the other placements had, for a while at least. They discussed the mental health problems Matthew had – and that helped. But he continued to be depressed and to also suffer occasional outbursts of manic energy.

Reading the book makes one thing very clear. Dealing with a troubled teenager is hell but being a troubled teenager is also hell. And the book does urge honesty. Tell the truth. While in care, Huggins discovered that the man he thought was his father was not his father, which provoked more depression and fury. It is also optimistic. Teenagers can get over their mental health problems. At the age of 21 Huggins became the youngest Councillor in Britain. It was not an immediate happy ending though. Under pressure from all kinds of politics, Huggins then became addicted to drugs and drink.

Finally Huggins got himself straight. At the end of the chapter, I reveal what happened to him.

Violence

Physical child abuse by stepfathers is frequent according to the NSPCC. Each week 600 new children come on to the official child- protection register in England and Wales; 26 per cent of all rapes are committed against children – often in stepfamilies. Canadian research shows that men behave very differently towards their biological children and their stepchildren. In family wipe-outs, discussed in Chapter 3, stepchildren are four times more likely to die at the hands of stepfathers than biological children are at the hands of their 'real' fathers.

Men who feel they cannot cope with stepfamily tensions should seek help.

In a stepfamily, everyone has to cope with new people who have new habits. In theory we should be able to treat this as an adventure. Authors of children's books are well aware of the distrust dynamic. A niche market has developed in books about how families 'blend'. In them, the steps are not the evil weirdos of fairy tales. *Living with My Stepfather is Like Living with a Moose* – good title, as Christopher Marlowe says to Shakespeare in *Shakespeare in Love* when he says he's got a play called *Ethel, the Pirate's Daughter* – and *The Stepman* have similar plots. The kids hate the stepfather but they come to accept he's not a monster. He does have odd habits but he does love their mother. Hugs, hot chocolate and happiness for everyone.

Winning trust is not easy, especially when children are hurt or confused. Stepfathers themselves have often been through experiences which make them mistrustful. Laying down rules may seem arrogant but there are two simple ones I believe stepfathers should follow.

Do not complain about the biological father even if their mother complains about him. With one big exception – if their real father is being abusive or violent.

It is not easy, but try to be consistent in the amount of emotion and warmth you offer. Do not be the committed stepdad one weekend and a week later act as if you had nothing much to do with them. That really can flake children out.

You may of course find your stepchildren are fun and then there is a real dilemma. How much of a father do you become to them? This can be especially difficult when the children are really small. Often, men have to find a difficult balance between not pretending to be the real dad and, yet, at the same time, being a good enough most of the time parent.

With small children, 'new families' battles are often practical as well as psychological. You and your new partner may have different styles of discipline. You may be an authoritarian 'my word is law' dad while your new partner's children are used to a permissive father. If you don't insist her children go to bed at 9 p.m. what happens when your kids come to stay? You can hardly tell them to go to bed if her children are staying up.

Self Analysis 11
Here are examples from real life which stepdads should ponder

What happens if dinner is fish pie? Fred hates fish pie. Do you cook something different for Fred?
Who gets to choose the TV we watch?
What are the rules about doing homework?
What are the rules about bedtime? In one family, six-year-olds go to bed at 9 p.m. and are never allowed to stay up later. In another, they go to bed at 8.30 but if there is something especially good on TV they can stay up later.
What are the rules about going into the parents' bedroom?

When you are trying to bring two families together, adults and children both need everything to be as clear as possible. Never easy, and harder still when a new stepfamily is starting because it is an emotional time. A National Institutes of Health (NIH) study found a stepfamily takes several years to develop into a real family unit. There is most risk of failure in the first two years because of muddles about what stepparents should do and what authority they have, conflicts between the parent the child is living with and the other parent, not to mention emotional and financial tensions.

Jealousy

For the child the situation is confusing. Children want attention; children get jealous. Are you, the stepfather, the man who is now spending the night in his mother's bed? Where his father used to be? Where, according to Freud, the boy fantasises unconsciously he wants to be? You don't kill your father because he is bigger and you have started to identify with him, but since your father probably wants your stepfather killed – I'm talking unconscious urges – in many cases, the child has every unconscious reason to be angry, even violent.

After separation or divorce, common sense says that parents should still work together to bring up their children. In 2000, Professor Jackie Walker of Newcastle University, who led a research programme for the Lord Chancellor's Department, warned lawyers and social workers not to be too optimistic about such co-operation. It is hard to achieve.

It's obviously helpful for stepparents and biological parents to communicate without bitterness so that they are consistent and back each other up in dealing with children. One useful idea is for stepfamilies to hold what I call *House Counsel and Curry*.

You are bribing the children but for a good reason: they need to listen and to have the chance to speak. Talking is the only solution. Order an Indian takeaway. If that's too expensive, agree with your partner to cook something special. It is an occasion. Get everyone relaxed and then explain the rules of the House Counsel and Curry; John B. Watson would have approved. Don't call it a family council because that allows her children to say 'where's my real daddy' and your children to say 'where's my real mummy?'

Explain that everyone needs to work out what the rules of living together in the new house are. Every house needs rules. You could do worse than use the issues of *Self Analysis 11* to start talking. If you can't agree, it will all end in tears and fighting. If the children are small, use dolls to play fight this disaster.

Then tell the children what you think are fair rules for the kinds of situations described in *Self Analysis 11* – which had to with TV, homework, eating, essentials of daily life. Others key issues are:

- What kinds of behaviour should be punished?
- How severely?
- What kind of behaviour should be praised or rewarded?

House Counsel and Curry gives children the chance to protest and it gives adults a chance to see what the kids think and then change their minds. If the children suggest something silly, laugh. But nothing should be off-limits. Very clever people easily forget decisions that have been agreed which is why the Cabinet keeps minutes. Do the same.

Once you have agreed House Rules, write up the Rules of the House on a notice board and get everyone to sign. It sounds silly, but it means kids have to commit to something.

This will help create an atmosphere in which children know talk and negotiation is possible. Promise yourselves to hold such a Council once a month because there are bound to be blow-ups in stepfamily life. Wise adults will agree a consistent position on some issues at least.

The worst problems in stepfamilies come, not surprisingly, when the family is not stable. The mother changes boyfriends, the children have to cope with one man after another. No one seems to have studied how single dads cope with children if they have a constant change of girlfriends. Someone should!

As there are many tensions, it's not surprising that some stepfathers hit on strange survival strategies. One of my favourites is Brian who has a website *How to survive as a stepdad*.

Brian says that, while he still loves his biological children, his first loyalty is now to his new woman. He has now become mature enough to be selfish. Brian only gets to see his biological child on weekends while his new mate and her child are there every day of the week. In Brian's view, at least, this justifies putting the needs of his new love ahead of those of his child.

Play fair

Piaget and Kohlberg (Kohlberg, 1984) found children have a sense of fairness. House Curry and Counsel should give children a chance to raise their problems at least.

If your Harriet is smacked when she is rude to her new stepmum, while her Tina gets away with just a telling off when she is rude to you, it will end in tears. The children will feel worse than confused. You will have raised some of the most painful spoken and unspoken questions in the stepfamily situation.

- Do you love me as much?
- Do you love him or her more?
- Why do you love me less?

These questions are at the root of most anguish. Avoid anguish by being loving and fair.

In a stepfamily all the children must feel they are equal and treated the same. Injustices don't help love grow. The theory is fine but putting it into practice – making all the children in a blended house feel they are loved, loved equally, and loved despite the fact that they are as different as chalk and cheese – needs patience, skill and, yes, real love. The truth is that you will almost certainly not love your stepchildren as much as your children. But you can make stepchildren feel secure – and make sure their mother shows them how much she loves them.

I return to the use of humour to defuse tension. If the children are small, use dolls to play games about a family that quarrels. If the children are older, invent a surreal stepfamily and describe in these family councils the tangles they get themselves in.

Self Analysis 12
Think about these questions:

In what kind of situations do you favour your children?
What annoys you about your stepchildren?
Are you likely to lose your temper more easily with your stepchildren than with your own children?
If so, what can you do about it?
What do you like about your stepchildren?
Is there any hobby or activity you can share with one or more of your stepchildren?
Would you rather live in a situation where they were not always there – getting between you and your new partner?

Putting yourself in a position where you have to choose between your partner and your children can lead to despair. You can't avoid some conflicts, but you can still be a good father, a good stepfather and a good new husband or new partner. I learned you need love, patience, negotiating skills, the occasional 'I am finally now going to put my foot down' and the also occasional ride to the rescue. You can't manage this if you're not prepared to be honest with yourself – and look at your behaviour.

People do not suddenly become saints but you need to analyse your behaviour scrupulously and see what you can do to change it. If your relationship with your new partner is good, you should be able to talk to her about these problems, as she is likely to have similar difficulties in coping with your own children.

The one day a week dad

Groups like *Families Need Fathers* stress the need for part-time fathers to be treated fairly by the law when it comes to access, child support and the education of the children. This

"You just wait until your father gets parental access."

Source: www.CartoonStock.com

is not a legal book and men who are divorcing or separating need good legal advice. At the end of the book, there is a list of useful organisations.

The part-time father may feel isolated and bitter. His life has been ruined by the divorce. He only sees his children once or twice a month. If he yells at his daughter during an access visit, he can't recover naturally in the course of daily life.

I found myself in the middle of access wars when one of my relatives split from the mother of his children. This young man drank too much, turned up late to pick up his son and once tried to bash the mother's door in because she would not let him in. He was drunk and late, she accused. Inevitably, it ended up in court.

Julia Ross and I offered our house as a safe place for visits. As Julia was then a director of social services the court allowed us to supervise visits. They were awkward at the beginning. Father and mother wouldn't say a word to each other. She insisted on waiting round the corner. The tense atmosphere upset their four-year-old son. It improved after the mother left but my relative resented being supervised by his family. He'd never hit his son. He couldn't be normal in our living room, he complained, but we had told the court we would supervise.

Slowly the relationship between father and son did get better – and visits do not have to be supervised now. Be willing to make concessions to avoid getting caught in a legal tangle if your ex has custody.

Often mothers will come round because they know children need to stay in touch with their father and for a less altruistic reason. Mothers need time by themselves for themselves. Stay in control, bottle up resentment and might have beens and try to find the strength to be generous in such fraught situations. Don't let yourself be isolated. Many other fathers are in the same difficult situation.

I've painted a rather bleak picture, but many step-families do succeed in the end. We need far more research into how to make stepfamilies work better because there will be more and more of them in the future. Some statistics predict that by 2030 no one will be living in an ordinary family with a mum, a dad and the children they have conceived together.

I promised to reveal what happened to Matthew Huggins. He now runs an organisation whose aim is to improve the way local authorities deal with children in care.

17

Can we see inside the teenage mind?

We tend to think teens are a twentieth-century phenom-
enon but the word was used as early as 1611, according to
the Oxford Dictionary; it then meant – rather appro-
priately – 'to anger, vex or cause to grieve'. By 1673, however, teenager had got its modern meaning, someone aged
between 13 and 19.

Just as 'teens' is not a new word, teenage tantrums are
not new. In the late Victorian best seller, *The Diary of a
Nobody*, Mr Pooter, the nobody, has to cope with his
18-year-old son, Loomis. Loomis has trouble with girls,
trouble with money and trouble with his get-rich-quick
schemes. Loomis would make a perfect twenty-first-century
teen because when he's broke, he's good at buttering up
mum and sponging off dad. Otherwise, he can't be
bothered. When Pooter gets him a job at the bank where
he works, Loomis makes mistakes, is rude to the bosses and
bunks off.

Many parents say they dread the teens because they
expect endless battles (Herbert, 1987) – battles about school,
dress, money, sex, telephone bills, staying out late and being
left alone – issues of control and privacy. How much do you,
as a parent, have the right to know about your children?
Parents usually think children belong to them and so they
have total rights. When children are eight years old that
is reasonable; when young people are 20 years old, it's
obviously false. At what point does protecting your children
become oppressing your children? Fathers need to think

about it because many parents hate not knowing everything about their children.

Pooter would have been surprised if he had ever met Piaget. According to Piaget, by the age of 14, the human child is a paragon of logic. Since Piaget had three children, I can only presume:

1 He never saw his children. Untrue.
2 His children were hypnotised. Untrue
3 A fairy sprinkled logic powder on Neuchatel where the Piagets lived or there was some secret ingredient in Swiss chocolate. Who knows?

At the age of 14, the Piaget child, the concrete operational child, becomes a mini Einstein! A master of logical or formal operations. Put an equation in front of your teenager like: 'What is implied by if P, then Q'.

Teenager quips 'Easy as pie' and 'Q with knobs on'. I have argued that Piaget under-estimated the capacities of young children, but he made up for that when it came to teens by seeing them as totally logical. Only 1 in 76 of us, in fact, ever attains Piaget's stage of formal operations and most of those become mathematicians or philosophers.

This chapter deals with normal teenagers, the 75 others out of the sample of 76. I imagined till recently that if a normal teenager were asked what 'If P, then Q' implies, said teenager would tell Piaget to impale himself on the nearest alp.

Then I came upon the work of Frank Farley and colleagues at Temple University who know everything about teens, logic and risks. They begin with statistics that make one worry.

Car accidents – Males and females of age 16–20 are at least twice as likely to be in car accidents as drivers between the ages of 20 and 50. Car accidents are the leading cause of death in the range of 15- to 20-year-olds. Roughly 30 per cent of all younger drivers who die had been drinking alcohol before the accident.

Sexually Transmitted Diseases (STDs) – More than 50 per cent of all new HIV cases occur below 25 years of

age. AIDS is the seventh leading cause of death in the 13-
to 24-year-old range. Every hour, about two teens contract
HIV. Three million young people are diagnosed with STDs
every year.

Alcoholism – 40 per cent of all adult alcoholics have
reported that their first drinking problems occurred during
their teens.

Gambling – One in ten teenagers gambles a great deal
– usually of course with parents' money.

The structure of the brain changes towards the end of
the teens, according to Magnetic Resonance Imaging
research. Going against the statistics they cite, Farley
and his colleagues suggest these brain changes help
teenagers become more logical. The normal teen is not
wild and fancy free; in fact, he tends to overestimate risks
and is as cautious as an old style bank manager. It is adults
who delude themselves they are more invulnerable to risks.
Farley and his colleagues (Reyna and Farley, 2006)
challenge: are teens *really* the ones who make poorer
judgment in risky situations? No. Piaget was right. Hail the
logical teen!

Julie Goldberg at the University of Chicago found teens
think that the delights of alcohol outweigh the risks associated with getting drunk. Teens know they will get legless,
get arrested and might even be beaten up or sexually
assaulted when drunk, but 'calculate' that boozing is too
satisfying for them to stay sober!

Farley and his colleagues claim most teens are what
they call 'risky-deliberators' – who rely on reasoning that is
age-appropriate and logical. They calculate benefits against
risks before doing something dangerous. If a friend
suggests they should steal computer games from a shop,
the 'risky-deliberator' does not do that without thinking. He
is an Einstein of crime and considers the probability of
being caught and arrested but decides the games are so
good the risks are worth it. They also calculate the police
probably won't catch them as they are too busy with
paperwork.

Farley claims that adults actually think more *illogically*
than teens and use *more intuition* when making decisions!

Self Analysis 13
Ask yourself:
*Do you expect your 12-year-old to tell you (i) that they are
going out, (ii) where they are going out to, (iii) when they
will be back?*
Did your parents expect that of you?
What do you do if your teenage kids will not talk to you?

We tend to assume all these woes will lead to endless fights.
It can but there is also evidence that teenagers generally
get on with their parents. In the 1970s, about 75 per cent of
teenagers admitted they had a good relationship with their
parents (Coleman, 1974). A small study 30 years on suggests this is not so improbable. Smetana and Metzger
(Smetana *et al.*, 2004) followed 95 African-American,
middle-class adolescents from the age of 13 to 18. They
studied 'developmental transitions'. Did going to college and
living semi-independently away from home affect relationships with parents?

Older teens said they were closer to their mothers than
to their fathers. Older girls reported more conflict with
their mothers than older boys, but arguments did not prevent the girls and their mothers staying close. They tangled
over chores, clothes, how late the girl could stay out, what
she wore and boyfriends. Despite the conflicts, mothers and
daughters were emotionally close. If the father was there
throughout the teens, it made for more positive relationships at the end of adolescence.

The most interesting conclusion is that parents of
teenagers should not fear conflicts too much. Rows when
teenagers were 13 to 16 did not make for 'disruptions' (the
researchers' word) or a bad relationship in the later teens.
Many fathers worry both about discipline and losing their
kids but Smetana and Metzger conclude:

> parents should not be concerned about minor (not very
> angry) disagreements in early and middle adolescence, as
> these do not have long-lasting negative effects on
> relationships. Parents should attempt to maintain close,
> supportive relationships with their adolescents, however,

as the positive quality of relationships earlier in adolescence influences relationships in late adolescence and young adulthood.

Good advice but not always easy to follow when Little Miss has dressed up very provocatively to go out on a date.

Never forget – teenagers are hormones.

Hormones are not logical

Teenagers sometimes feel they don't know what their body is going to do next. Hormonal changes lead to growth spurts, facial hair, and acne; in boys the voice breaks. Many of us can remember feeling awkward and gawky as teenagers. Now there is even more pressure to look 'cool', well, cool isn't cool anymore so lets say 'trendy'. In the Netherlands, there is a vogue for plastic surgery for children and teens. Yet, as ever, there are individual differences. Some 13-year-old girls take pride in having large breasts; others find it embarrassing. The market for anti-acne products is huge – and boys worry about spots and pimples as much as girls. Parents have to learn to be sensitive and prepare for the following kinds of dialogue:

Parent: You look nice.
Teen: What do you know? Who cares what you think?

Fathers have to get ready to negotiate. Remember you have negotiated more than your kids. You should have an advantage.

I'm staying out, dad

Andrew and Cathy have five children. He is a police officer; she is a senior social work manager. Their oldest daughter is 13. They live in the countryside near north London. 'Emma is very horse oriented these days so we see little of her,' Andrew told me. Andrew and Cathy had recently had to put their foot down. They had been invited to a party. Emma was going out with friends. Andrew and Cathy had no idea that their daughter would change her plans.

In the middle of the party, Emma rang her parents on their mobile. She didn't want to come home that night. She wanted to spend the night in a field camping with some friends. A little questioning – Andrew is a policeman, after all – revealed that these friends included some older boys. Andrew and Cathy didn't think that a very good idea. They were worried about some of the boys. They told their daughter they would be back by 11.30 and they expected to see her home by then. 'We do lead by example,' Andrew said. They didn't mind curtailing their social life to make the point that Emma also had to be in by 11.30.

I asked Andrew if he thought he would behave the same way when Emma was a 15–16-year-old. He said he was not sure. I also asked him if he would have behaved the same way if Emma had been a boy. He thought about it a little and said 'yes' because the issue for him was being able to trust his child.

The negotiation between Emma and her parents is one of thousands that will take place during the teens. At 15 or 16, young people resent such controls usually and evade them by the simple device of not ringing their parents to say plans have changed. Parents need eternal patience when they are faced by an angry teenager.

Hell hath no fury like a verbal teenager

Since the age of ten, Josie (not her real name) had worried her teachers and her mother because she got so angry. Josie had no idea why she did. She had been admitted to Prestwich Adolescent Unit. I met her as a bright, mouthy 13-year-old who was fed up with all the 'talk' in the unit. Her mother was grossly overweight, had no partner and no work; she was on benefit, a woman with her own problems.

Therapists sometimes say that the problem is that problem children can't express their feelings. That was not Josie's problem; she could say what was bothering her loud, clear and clever. She was angry and bored and bored and angry.

Josie complained – and she could have won the Euro-vision Song Contest for Complaining – that she wasn't having much of a life. The high point of her week was to visit Tesco. And what was the point of going to a shop when she didn't have money to spend? When her mother came to visit, they had a going-in-circles row. Josie wanted £2.79 to buy fags; her mother refused to give it to her. Josie started tearing her clothes up. Her mother told her not to do that.

Josie kept on tearing her clothes up. Her mother said that was no way to get pocket money.

Josie calculated that her mother owed her pocket money and that, anyway, her mother was saving money. While Josie was in the Unit, Mum spent less on food. Josie said her mother loved her three sisters more. I wonder what Piaget would have made of that response. It's logically absurd and psychologically very smart. I save you money – you love me less.

The mother said she was fed up with Josie and just wanted to know what was wrong with her.

Josie and her mother are engaged in an extreme teenage battle. Josie is 'lucky' in that she has not been put on medication – probably because she is very articulate as well as provocative. And the person she provokes most is her mother, not the staff.

Teenage sex and vanity

Teenage insecurity often makes for teenage vanity. I shaved off one of my pimples when I was 14 to stop looking like Frankenstein's cousin. I then had to cover the scar which did not stop bleeding. I also became convinced I was going bald. So no girl would ever have sex with me if I had no hair and spots.

For dads the problem of the sexuality of their children, especially of their daughters, is not simple. Children are becoming sexual much younger than in the past. Girls start to develop breasts somewhere between eight and nine; many start to grow pubic hair when they are nine years old. The average age for the first period is 12–13 years as against 15–16 in the 1850s. We have better hygiene and nutrition to thank, experts say. There are now grandmothers in their mid-thirties, girls who gave birth when they were 16 and whose daughters gave birth when they too were 16. In such a family a girl could become a great-grandmother at 48 and, thanks to fertility treatment, have another baby herself!

Boys go into puberty later than girls but they too are doing so younger than a century ago.

Self Analysis 14
Ask yourself:
Did you ever talk about sex with your parents?
Would you have confided in them?
If the answer is no – which is true for most of the population – why should your kids confide in you?

There are many surveys of teenage sexual behaviour in Britain, America, Japan and other countries but subjects tend to exaggerate. They want to look good, to please the interviewer, not to look like a naïve dolt. So figures need to be viewed with caution especially as London is not representative of all Britain.

Studies in the 1970s found that 15 per cent to 18 per cent of teenagers claimed to have had sex before they reached 16. Thirty years later, a survey of 3,000 London teenagers aged 15–18 by The Trust for the Study of Adolescence found not much had changed; 18 per cent of teenagers said they had had sex before 16, the age of consent.

Other findings are worrying because they suggest that young sex involves too much pressure; 39 per cent had sex for the first time when one or other partner was not equally willing. Almost three in ten girls lost their virginity for 'negative reasons', such as wanting to please a boyfriend.

51 per cent of girls and 37 per cent of boys had had unprotected sex.

58 per cent of girls and 39 per cent of boys had slept with someone at least once without using a condom.

Two in five wish they had waited longer before having sex.

Only 20 per cent when they have sex for the first time take precautions, are in a steady relationship or feel the timing is right.

CosmoGirl magazine backed the report's call for Sex and Relationships Education to be made compulsory in schools to help tackle 'widespread knowledge gaps'.

The 1994 study *Sex and America's Teenagers* found 53 per cent of boys had had intercourse by their 18th birthday as against 26 per cent in the 1960s (Hine, 1999); 54 per cent of girls lost their virginity by the age of 18 as against 23 per cent in the 1960s. But since 1994, teen sex has been in decline which some attribute to the increasing influence of religion. The percentage of high school students in 2007 who had had sexual intercourse has declined by 12 per cent since 1991 and 20 per cent fewer had had sex with four or more partners. There has been a 7 per cent decline in the number of teenagers who were currently sexually active (Centers for Disease Control and Prevention, 2005).

Fathers and daughters

Freud did not look at why some fathers become too possessive of their daughters perhaps because of his own dependency on his youngest daughter, Anna. It is normal for fathers to fret when daddy's darling starts to have boyfriends which is perfectly normal teen behaviour. And fretting can lead to rows. When fathers complain their daughters wear too much make up and too few clothes, daughters fight back and insist they'll stay out as long as they want with whoever they want. Many fathers find that hard to handle for good and bad reasons. The good reason is that you want your daughter to be happy and safe; the bad reason is jealousy and wanting to control your daughter's life totally. Again you have to be ready to talk about this.

The only research on this subject is not direct, however. It looks at whether girls who report abuse felt their fathers were jealous of them when they had boyfriends. Not surprisingly, over 80 per cent said they felt their fathers were jealous. Unfortunately, this is not a normal sample – the girls had been abused.

It's a sign of the times that one of the great romantic comedy hits of the last ten years has been *Sleepless in Seattle*. It's the story of a young father who has lost the wife he adored. He has to look after his son on his own and the son decides his dad needs a new wife. In the past, no son would have dared think that or do something about it – especially as the boy is just eight years old! I apologise for the constant hair-theme but in 2009 there is an ad on TV in Britain where two girls insist their father dye his white hair grey so that he can get a date. 'You'd be a catch' they say with a grin. We presume dad has been dumped by their mum. The ad is cautious; there are two girls because if one daughter said that to him it would raise spectres of child sexual abuse.

How to improve your dad

I like *Sleepless in Seattle* because, as a father, I too had to cope with kindness though not, thank God, my children setting me up on dates. Boys don't go in for that. I found that teenage children and stepchildren lectured me on my many deficiencies. No research has been done into this maddening development. Here are some of the subjects of lectures:

Do you realise that you are eating too much red meat, dad?

Do you ever count how much booze you consume?

I'm thinking of going back to karate, dad, wouldn't that be a good thing for you to do? I don't mean to mention your paunch but . . . your paunch. A run before breakfast wouldn't kill you.

I am so worried about you dad!

It's all spoken with real love too.

I feel secure in the love of my children. I have no doubt they want the best for me. That seems to give them the right to dissect all my failings. I love them to bits, nevertheless, which means I listen, or half listen at least.

The teenage turning point

The psychoanalyst, Erik Erikson, argued adolescence was a turning point. In one's teens, one should resolve issues of identity versus role confusion. If teenagers did not try out different identities, they faced the dangers of being 'frozen' and of being stuck as 'immature personalities'. The boy who decides at 12 that he is going to be a pilot like Dad, or a teacher like Dad, may stop growing up psychologically and live in the shadow of his parents for ever. He's the boy who becomes a man like Tom, a pudgy cab driver, who lived with his mother till she died. She was 83 when she died; he was 62. He had never left home, never made an adult relationship and was devastated by her death.

By the age of 20, Erikson believed, the well adjusted young person should have made key decisions – are they heterosexual, what studies will they pursue, what are their aims in life? In the process, teenagers often tried out various identities and roles.

Just like they did in kindergarten!

I want to explore this possibly outrageous comparison which since authors are as vain as teenagers, is mine, all mine. We've seen how toddlers switch from pretending to be Batman to playing show-and-tell in the Wendy House. As they play and pretend, toddlers learn – how to co-operate, what the limits of 'decent' behaviour are, what other people's attitudes are and much else. Erikson talked of resolving role confusions and there is a superficial similarity between teenagers trying out who they are and toddlers pretending to be Batman and Supergirl. But teenagers don't see themselves as playing games. For them, it is serious and they are often self conscious about it.

One way to define what you are is to make it clear what you are against. If you're not sure what you are against, you can try out various options. But there's one big difference between the toddler and the teenager. Parents love little children and their monkey-like 'frolickings', Montaigne noted. Dad and mum coo and goo when their three-year-old swirls a black cape round their shoulder and announces 'I'm Matrix Minx'. How can her little brain be so imaginative, bless it! You don't get the same adoring response if you are a 14-year-old in Grub gear who lectures their parents on the virtues of vegan, why they should fight global warming and stop driving so that the earth does not smog up.

Partly it is about control. Teenagers can storm out of the house, disappear overnight to their friends and freak you out with worry. Here's the bad news. Pray your teen is not studying law. They might discover parents have fewer legal rights than one might think. At 16, children become adults for most legal purposes. They can marry without their parents' consent. You have no right to open their mail and listen to their phone conversations. The only right you have is to pay for all their clothes, food, entertainment and gadgets.

I started this book reporting the case of Umberto versus Dad who would not pay for his son to become a hairdresser. In another landmark case, The European Court of Human Rights ruled it is a violation for parents to ask 13-year-olds certain questions like 'where are you going tonight and how are you getting home?'

The family album

I have among our family photographs a picture of my mother with her parents. My mother must have been in her mid- to late-twenties. Her head is resting on her father's shoulder; she's smiling. It's a touching picture of an affectionate daughter. What's disturbing is the space between the two of them, the father–daughter couple and her mother, Teresa, my grandmother. Teresa stares out, not looking at either of them, a woman totally apart from the other two. The physical affection, the head on the shoulder, is all my mother's. When I look at that photograph, I'm often touched but I also remember my father accusing my mother of being too involved with her parents. She could never be a good wife, he stormed, because she had never really left home emotionally. She was always Daddy's girl, even years after Daddy died. It was like so many accusations in marriages – true and not true.

Setting boundaries is important at all ages and stages but perhaps particularly in the teens. But you can't set boundaries arbitrarily. And tact is required.

I wnt 2 b a loan – Greta Garbo

One kind of row seems to me also exceptionally hard to deal with, and I find it curious that surveys never seem to discuss it. I call these the Garbo rows in honour of Garbo's famous cry 'I want to be alone' – here spelled normally for the discerning. Her cry is relevant in the light of a 2008 finding that one third of British teenagers spend virtually no time with their parents. Parents want the teenager to be with them while teen-monster spends hours locked away in their room listening to music, watching TV, watching MTV, chatting online or playing computer games.

Long before you could iPod on the internet or 'txt', Gunter and McAleer (1990) found that, in the UK, the average teenager spends over 20 hours a week in front of the television. And, then, the more sociable teen is off with his or her mates – or gang. Teen-ology is not an exact science. One third of teens never see their parents; the other two thirds are always ready to lecture mum and dad on what they've done wrong.

Self Analysis 15
Ask yourself:
Were you isolated as a teenager?
Did you cut off?
Was it shyness? Or did you just feel quite misunderstood?
Who were your heroes/heroines as a teen?
How can you use some of this to talk to your own teen?

Why do teenagers want to be alone? This is one of the many mysteries of life psychologists have yet to answer.

The only two things you can do is let them know you are there and not to nag.

Parent: I need to talk to you.

Teenager is silent. Teenage glares the Silent Stare, the Silent Sulk, the head down in my lap top, the door slam, the don't you ask where I am dragon in the lair look, and then storms out.

But you are not defenceless. I also recommend singing to your teenager if you really want to irritate them:

You're not cool
Dad's no fool
Don't be cruel.

18

Stress and mental health

Remember *Star Wars* and the Princess with the weird hairdo that looked like a doughnut? She was played by Carrie Fisher who was the daughter of Debbie Reynolds, herself a star. Carrie Fisher got hooked on drugs and ended up spending some time in rehab. In those days no one had heard of celebrity rehab – special clinics for the specially famous. The first decade of the twenty-first century saw the growth of celebrity rehab. Graduates of celebrity rehab – well, some cynics aren't sure they've graduated yet – include Amy Whitehouse and Britney Spears.

Being the father of a rock star may seem glamorous but it seems to involve a great deal of rescuing. Some of it may be fun but a lot of it will be a nightmare.

Addiction is only one of the many nightmares parents can face. Many dads hate to realise they can't protect their children from everything. And that leads to problems. There are no easy answers if your child is very sick, shows signs of mental illness or addiction or has joined a genuinely frightening gang. Anyone who offers them is being glib.

Gangs and mental health

In September 2008, Channel 4 News reported on gangs in south London. Social workers and policemen argued that many black youngsters on rough estates did not have good role models. Their fathers had decamped or were in jail, so the boys had no one to teach them how to be a man. In

America 27 million kids suffer from father absence. David Carr Brown in his films *A Chronicle of Violence*, which looked at gangs in Paris suburbs, came to much the same conclusion.

Gangs are a serious problem in London. More teenagers were killed in the city than ever before in 2007 as there were 26 murders, nearly double the figure for 2006. Even before that, Lemos (2004) found one in ten boys aged 11 and 12 carried a knife or other weapon, of whom 8 per cent admitted intending to inflict serious harm. Scotland Yard's Violent Crime Directorate believe at least 171 gangs operate in London – and some have more than 100 members.

Fathers must not ignore such issues and need to try and talk to their children about them.

Giles (not his real name) is a barrister. He said:

> I was very shocked when I discovered my daughter had been bunking off school. I felt worried for her and guilty that I didn't know. My mother who should have known better to some extent colluded but I knew my daughter was taking drugs and that she was drinking far too much. I was never sure whether to confront her or to collude. I would give her money and she would spend it on drink and drugs which didn't make her feel any better. She could be charming but she was often very cut off. I didn't shut my eyes but all I could do was tell her I was there. It did not feel good at the time. I was scared. When she went out, I often caught myself waiting, listening for the sound of the door banging when she was back home.

In heart-breaking situations, fathers need to balance concern and panic. The nonchalant dad – 'I am too cool to ever worry' – may miss danger signs. But panic will not help either. You need to keep battling with energy, hope, intelligence, common sense and love.

After many attempts, Giles' daughter stopped drinking. She has now lost a stone and feels better about herself. Giles still tends to be too anxious and his daughter complains that all too often he behaves as if she were 13, not

18. He knows that irritates her but it doesn't make it easy for him to stop worrying.

Drink and drugs

Some parents get upset if their children smoke the occasional joint, but hardly worry if they drink four pints of lager. According to the Home Office in 2000, 50 per cent of under-15s had tried cannabis and 15 per cent had tried ecstasy.

A survey of 2,000 teenagers carried out by the European School Survey Project on Alcohol and Other Drugs for 2004 found that 42 per cent of boys and 35 per cent of girls admitted they had tried illegal drugs at least once. The figures apply to Europe as a whole.

The British Crime Survey 2005/2006 estimated that 34.9 per cent of 16- to 59-year-olds have used one or more illicit drugs; 10.5 per cent used one or more illicit drugs in the last year, and 6.3 per cent in the last month. Cannabis is the most used: 8.7 per cent of 16- to 59-year-olds reported using cannabis in the last year. In America the statistics are that 36 per cent of 17-year-olds used it in the past year. The British Crime Survey reports that one person in every 40 claims to have used cocaine in the past year.

Morally, I have no problem with cannabis. I never had any issue with my children smoking small amounts of it – occasionally – but crack, cocaine and heroin were different. I worry because many teenagers flash their bravado. Of course I can do drugs, dad, I know them back to front.

Since the 1970s, governments all over the world have tried to monitor the 'quality' of drugs sold on the street and failed, except possibly in Holland. Most drug dealers want to make as much money as possible so they sometimes mix drugs with different substances, like washing powder. In a black market, the buyer can hardly complain if he gets second-rate heroin.

The *Liverpool Daily Post* (27 October 2007) reported parents 'are naïve and complacent about the widespread use of cannabis among teenagers'. Merseyside Assistant Chief Constable Simon Byrne complained that 'frankly there is a group of parents that are complacent and turn a blind eye to drug use in the sense of "out of sight, out of mind" and in turning that blind eye, they are creating a deeper mess because we are worried about the rise in potency of the cannabis on the streets'. The government agreed and, in 2009, made cannabis a Class B rather than a Class C drug.

I found the Liverpool report sad and ironic. I made a film for ITV in 1985 called *Kicking The Habit* which looked at the work of a group of parents on the Wirral (which is part of Merseyside). They were campaigning against drug use because they were so scared for their teenagers. They were pushing the kids into counselling. More than 20 years later their efforts had not helped the problem in Merseyside.

Occasional use of cannabis is one thing. Regular use is utterly different because there is evidence that it affects cognitive performance. It is worrying and frightening whether your child is addicted to cannabis, cocaine, heroin or alcohol.

Be prepared to be personal. Today's dads may well have tried drugs. I told my kids I had done so. Some drugs had been quite nice – mescalin made me see the world in an agreeable blur – but some had terrified me. Once I was sure mini-policemen were crawling out of the toilet and about to arrest me. There was a block of police flats nearby. I was never a regular user, but I think it was not a bad thing to let my children know I had some idea both of the attractions and the dangers of drugs. This may seem controversial but I do believe in being truthful to your children.

If you feel concerned try to persuade them to seek help with you. My late father-in-law gave me a good example of this. He was appalled when he discovered one of his sons had a bad drug problem but he went to a number of coun-selling sessions with him. It did not immediately do the trick, but I believe it played some part in persuading his son to sort himself out. For my father in law, it was an agonising process and, sadly, he died before his son got out of the mess and misery his dependency had caused. The son is now a successful lawyer and devoted father of two.

Booze, booze, booze

In 1998, a third of children under 14 drank alcohol. Nine years later the problem was worse according to two different British studies. The Scottish Schools Adolescent Lifestyle and Substance Use Survey (SALSUS) reported some alarming findings in 2006: 35 per cent of 15-year-old boys and 37 per cent of 15-year-old girls reported drinking in the past week. Among 13-year-olds, 13 per cent of boys and 15 per cent of girls had taken alcohol in the previous week; 15-year-old boys said they had consumed an average of 18 units of alcohol in the previous week; 13-year-old boys and girls both reported drinking an average of 13 units in the previous week. 47 per cent of 13-year-olds and 63 per cent of 15-year-olds had been drunk in the previous seven days. Most said they had been drunk at least ten times in their short lives.

In April 2007, Srabani Sen, Chief Executive of Alcohol Concern, said 'we are simply not doing enough to protect our children from alcohol'. At present you can give a child as young as five alcohol in your own home. Sen wanted that raised to 15. Home Office research shows that a third of underage boys and girls can buy alcohol in pubs and bars.

Alcohol damages children's performance at school – and worse. Around 14 per cent of pupils excluded from school were suspended for drinking. Yet schools teach little about what is a serious problem, Sen argues.

It is always a nasty shock when you realise your child is drinking too much and much better if you can spot the problem before you find them coming home late reeking of booze. Apart from drink disappearing from your cupboard and your teen smelling of booze, watch for:

- excessive moodiness
- rudeness
- mood swings
- money disappearing mysteriously.

The most depressing feeling is if you feel you no longer know your child or can talk to him or her.

If you think your child is drinking alone in his or her bedroom, try to ask about it. Don't storm in to confront but don't ignore it either – a balance that is not easy to achieve. It is never simple to persuade a surly, secretive teenager out of the bedroom, but a mix of patience, humour and insistence can achieve it. They love you too, remember.

Don't, really don't, lose your temper and say things like 'if you ever do that again I'll throw you out of the house'. Teenagers do sometimes leave home for good after such rows.

Fat is not just a feminist issue now

The National Institute for Eating Disorders claims that in the UK some 60,000 people are suffering from some sort of eating disorder – either anorexia or bulimia. Glamorous, thin models don't help because they encourage girls not to eat. There are fierce controversies about causes. The therapist Susie Orbach in *Fat is a Feminist Issue* argued low self esteem was a major cause. In a celebrity-crazed society, where you can't afford to look bad, teenage boys have also started to develop eating disorders.

In America, pessimists claim 15,000 people a year die from eating disorders but optimists say it is just 950. Whatever the true statistics, the problem is serious.

Tony (not his real name) is a policeman in the North of England and divorced. His 14-year-old daughter often returns from staying with her mother and refuses to eat. Tony gets very worried and takes time off work to stay with her. He has not found it easy to find help. Social services did send someone to see him but the visitor was not even a social worker. As a policeman Tony knows local resources but even so he did not manage to get his daughter to see a doctor for 48 hours at a time when he felt the situation was desperately urgent.

Since Tony's daughter was being difficult, as teenagers with eating disorders are, she refused to be weighed. He felt helpless.

If your child is suffering from anorexia or bulimia you need professional help as soon as possible. And you also need to make sure it is appropriate. Thousands of girls and boys do recover usually with counselling. Be careful you don't accentuate the problem by nagging a child to eat. Anorexics have strong wills and are likely to win a battle of wills even if it is self-destructive. Get help.

Medication

Very worryingly in the twenty-first century, more and more children are being medicated partly because no one seems to have better solutions. Joseph Bierdermann, professor of psychiatry at Harvard, has been criticised for diagnosing children as young as two as suffering from bipolar disorder and recommending they be treated with a cocktail of drugs. Senator Charles Greeley (who is a Republican) and Alison Bass, a respected American journalist, have investigated these trends. What makes them worse is that small children are being treated with drugs designed for adults but that have not been tested on children or approved for use on them (*New York Review of Books*, 15 January 2009). The practice is not illegal incidentally but few people realise it goes on both in the States and Britain.

More and more British children are also being put on medication. Psychiatrists sometimes admit that one reason for prescribing medication is that a young person causes so much anxiety to his or her parents. There is no other way to cope, it seems. Child psychiatry is badly resourced with only about 600 beds in psychiatric units in Britain specially designed for the under-16s. In 2008, many teenagers were put in adult psychiatric wards. Everyone agrees this is imperfect, the government has promised more resources but many children still do not get proper help. It is estimated – and I stress the word estimated because the statistics are elusive – that 80,000 under-16s are on antidepressants and antipsychotics in the UK.

In a short term crisis, medication can help and even save life. But, all too often, GPs just repeat prescriptions because 'everyone' is frightened of the child being out of control if she or he is taken off drugs. And prescribed drugs can be as addictive as illegal ones.

Be careful before you consent to your child going on medication. Always talk to your child. She or he has rights. If necessary, consult an organisation like MIND. Always ask for a second opinion.

Talk till you are blue in the face

If you see your child is unhappy, talk. It will not be easy if they are hostile but keep on trying. Hopefully by the time they get to their teens, your child will know you really love and want the best for them.

If your child seems no longer like himself or herself, you need to consider the following:

Is your child eating properly?
Is there any reason to fear your child is showing signs of an eating disorder?
Is he or she being bullied at school?
Is she or he scared of failing at school?
Is he or she worried you may be going to divorce?
Does your child seem depressed?
Is there any reason to suspect they are self harming?
Does one child feel you love another child more?
Does he or she hate their brother/sister/stepbrother for some reason?
Is she worried because she may be pregnant?
Has your child started to take drugs?

John B. Watson was right; children need to talk and can talk. Fathers and mothers have to get them in the habit from the very start and do their best to keep them talking. If there is a crisis, it's obviously easier to talk if you are a family that talks anyway. If you are a family where the children lock themselves in their rooms, getting them to talk will be the first crisis before you start dealing with the true crisis. But if you have always talked as a family, you should not get into that kind of stand off.

Be patient. Give a child time to respond.
If you ask questions, keep them open-ended.
Do not lose your cool, your temper, your rag.

Do not assume you know what is wrong with your child. They are an independent person in their own right. That is not, really not, an easy rule to keep especially as you may be frightened your child is going to be in trouble with the law.

Paternal guilt and insight

Guilt is a problem when your children seem to be troubled. If you are inclined to guilt, advice in a book is unlikely to change you. But ask yourself why you feel guilty and, crucially, is your guilt helping. Guilt often makes bad situations worse; those who suffer from it can become resentful and 'passive aggressive'.

Suggesting you don't wallow in guilt does not mean you should not ask yourself difficult questions if your child is in distress. The questions are not ones I have liked asking of myself at times.

Self Analysis 16
Ask yourself:
Have I been doing anything which is making my kid feel so bad? That involves trying to talk very openly with your child and examining your own behaviour.
Have I been too harsh or impatient?
Have I been so obsessed with my work or other things that I have not given my child enough time for their problems?
Do I show my child how much I care?
What could I do that will make my child feel better about herself or himself?

The ideas of therapist Carl Rogers may help. He believed in giving his patients total attention and support and termed this 'unconditional personal regard'. It is one thing to do this for the therapeutic hour and quite another to do it day in day out. But you could try giving that to a child for an hour a day twice or three times a week. (If the kid is old enough, explain why you are doing this. You both need help in the relationship.) One of the first rules of medicine is don't do harm. It is hard to see how really giving a kid complete attention for an hour could do any harm.

It is not easy for any father to question how he is parenting, but such questions are necessary if you want to help your child in a crisis.

19

The worst: depression, attempted suicide, suicide

An eight-year-old girl lay screaming on the floor of a consulting room at Stanford University Medical Center. She was kicking and fighting with nurses and doctors because she just did not want them to touch her. She was about to undergo a painful procedure that was medically necessary but thoroughly humiliating.

The girl had a rare hereditary urinary-tract defect. Every year the doctors had to check whether urine was backing up into the girl's kidneys. They were about to insert a catheter through her urethra into the bladder, inject a dye, and have the girl urinate while being X-rayed.

I remember feeling powerless as a father every time one of my boys had to go to the doctors.

We will return to the Medical Center after looking at some even more desperate problems fathers can face.

In 2001, James Lawson killed his daughter who was desperately depressed. She begged him to help her die because she could no longer take it after years of suffering. Her father suffocated her. Lawson was given a suspended sentence on the grounds of diminished responsibility. Passing sentence, the judge said he could not imagine a more tragic crime.

Ten-year-old Dijendra was bullied at school and hanged himself. His family were surprised and blamed the school for failing to protect him. The inquest at Southwark returned an open verdict. Dijendra was not one isolated young death.

In 2005, 28 children under the age of 14 (10 girls and 18 boys) took their lives in England and Wales and 71 who were under 18. In the previous year it had been 92. One in 12 children and young people deliberately self harm according to the Child and Adolescent Mental Health Survey (2004). The Samaritans state that more than 24,000 teenagers are admitted to hospital in the UK each year as a result of deliberately harming themselves (Samaritans and Centre for Suicide, University of Oxford, 2002).

The tragedy of child and adolescent suicide hits every culture. In 2003 there was an international conference on child and teenage suicide. In Singapore, a society which is very achievement orientated, 28 children had killed themselves in 2001, nearly all of them by jumping from balconies in high rise blocks. The youngest victim was a nine-year-old girl.

Dr Daniel Fung of the University of Singapore admitted that he had imagined that these young people killed themselves because of poor grades in school. He and his colleagues were surprised to find in fact the main cause was not related to school; it was stress over relationships with parents, boyfriends or girlfriends. School failure was a possible 'trigger' in just three suicides. The Samaritans of Singapore reported two thirds of the callers under 19 were troubled by problems with family members.

One tragedy families bitterly regret later is that often those who kill themselves have uttered a 'cry for help'. David Shaeffer of Columbia University, an expert on teenage suicide, said most suffer from depression for six months to two years before their deaths. Shaeffer found two factors trigger teenage suicides: getting into trouble, such as cheating, and losing a boyfriend or girlfriend.

Parents can become exhausted by their teenager's constant attempts to get attention by misbehaving. Twenty years ago, I interviewed Rebecca who was then in her late teens. She had made 13 suicide attempts. She felt better after she had cut herself. One attempt had its black funny side. Rebecca had walked topless into the sea at Clacton, yelling 'Jimmy I'm coming to join you.' Jimmy was her husband who, as Rebecca's mother acidly pointed out, had managed to kill himself at his first attempt. Jimmy threw himself with perfect timing under a tube train. Rebecca seemed to make sure there was always someone on hand to save her.

On Clacton beach, the will-Rebecca-die-or-not saga drew police, the coastguard and an audience of gawping spectators. Rebecca was dragged out of the sea. She told the story with some irony at her own expense. But her mother couldn't see the humour. She was too tired. Rebecca had got what she wanted as usual, even more attention than usual.

In Britain nearly 850,000 children and young people have a mental disorder – one child in every ten (Office for National Statistics Child and Adolescent Mental Health Survey, 2004).

Peter Wilson who founded the mental health charity Young Minds, argues children face 'problems that are more complicated, more extreme, more pressing and children seem to be more agitated, more fractious, more disorganised and are not sure where they are'.

Many consultant child psychiatrists agree. Dr Andrew Clark, a consultant at the Prestwich Adolescent Unit, told me:

> Children from eight years upwards can give an account of a depressive episode. They feel horrible inside, they feel their friends think they're no good, they don't want to get up in the morning, life isn't worth living. Unless you talk to the young people you don't get these accounts. Parents and teachers are very good at telling what young people do and don't do but they're not good at telling you how it feels inside that young person.

And some teenagers who feel unheard will self harm. It is not just a cry for attention, some do die (Crowell *et al.*, 2004). They write: 'There is no better predictor of suicide than previous suicide attempts.' They also comment on a discovery. Brain chemistry can exacerbate the problem. A low level of serotonin, one of the neurotransmitters in the brain, seems to make it easier to self harm.

Crowell and Beauchaine studied 20 self harming adolescents (average age 15 years) and compared them with 21 controls. Teenagers filled out questionnaires about their mental health, self harming, and family conflicts. The researchers then picked a topic that caused stress – doing chores. Helping with the washing up turned out to be explosive as 'within five minutes some of our subjects were arguing with each other'. About the ironing, the washing and who cleans the toilet! After ten minutes of what was usually mayhem, the teenagers gave a blood sample. The researchers could now assess their hormones and, especially, their serotonin level. The result was surprising.

There was a strong link between low levels of serotonin and the girls' self harming but there were also links which have nothing to do with biochemistry. Teenagers who experience much conflict with their mothers are much more likely to harm themselves. Destructive behaviour can become addictive. 'Once self-harming behavior starts it is difficult to stop. Over time, with something such as cutting, children's bodies react to it in a way that helps reduce biological and psychological pain. They essentially become addicted to this behavior. So you want to prevent this behavior before it starts,' Crowell and Beauchaine wrote.

But prevention is not easy. There is first of all a lack of services and then even when children get treatment, depression is not something that is easy to treat. At the Prestwich Unit, while making a film called *The Madness of Children* for Channel 4, I interviewed Judy and Susan. Judy had been admitted after trying to kill herself. She was an articulate 18-year-old. I recorded a discussion she had with Kate Kellett, the art therapist, and two other girls about self harm:

> *Judy:* I just do it because I hate myself and I think I deserve it.
> *Kate:* You deserve to be punished in what way?
> *Judy:* Yeah.
> *Kate:* That's different from the way it's for you.

She looked at Susan as she said that. Susan was not that obviously depressed but her wrists and lower arms were pitted – slashes, cuts, damage. She said it was always voices she heard that triggered her self harm. Earlier in the week Susan asked Kate to get razors for her. Kate had refused. Judy pointed out the obvious; 'She's supposed to help so how would you feel if she just said "Go for it"?'

> *Susan:* In the long run I know it's bad but in the short term, given the way that I feel now, I'd think thank God here's someone who understands how what's going on.
>
> *Judy:* I know it's a solution but it's not the solution to get you better.
>
> *Kate:* You know that, don't you?
>
> *Susan:* There's a bit of me that knows that it's not right but then the voices start saying to me and the bigger part of me say you know you've got to do it. It's an impossible situation. It's incredibly hard to stop once you've done it. Even if I didn't do for years I'd always have to come back to it eventually.

Susan made a lumpy clay figure later on and smiled. For her, this figure was 'like a guardian . . . There are so many bad guys . . . We could do with some good guys to help me to fight the voices. It makes me feel good, helping to create someone who could help me. I know he can't really but it feels like it could help,' she said.

Frightening voices

Voices are a key symptom of schizophrenia and psychiatrists used to believe there were few cases of schizophrenia before the age of 16. Now, children have psychotic breakdowns much younger.

When 14-year-old Sarah went to Brookside, a therapeutic community just outside Romford, she presented classic schizophrenic symptoms including frightening voices that she refused to describe. The clinic slowly unravelled a traumatic and confused background.

Sarah had seen her father die and blamed herself for his death. It was not clear whether her mother also blamed her for her father's death. Sarah's voices started then. Her mother mourned the death of her husband, but eventually she did make a new relationship. It didn't work well as he was violent. Sarah saw her mother being beaten up by the new bloke and blamed herself for her mother being beaten up. Sarah disliked the man but there was nothing to suggest he disliked her, or abused her.

Paul Caviston, Brookside's consultant psychiatrist, told me that there were, of course, many children who saw men being violent to their mothers. But many children who experience such family traumas cope and do not start hearing voices. Just what makes the difference remains something of a mystery.

Susan's feelings were diagnosed as depression. Her despair, anger and a need for release are easy to describe and Hell to live through. Thousands of teenagers are hit by such bleak black moods and often they can't pinpoint what triggers them.

The conference in Singapore gave researchers from all over the Far East the chance to recommend preventative measures. The trigger, the final straw that pushes a teen over the edge is not easy to spot and if parents miss it, they are likely to blame themselves very badly. There are, however, tell-tale signs of a teen near the brink which parents need to be alert to if they feel their child is vulnerable. These are sudden changes of behaviour, a loss of interest in once favourite activities, bad school results. The Singapore Conference pointed to the obvious. 'The must-not-ignore signs are when they write farewell notes, call up friends to say goodbye, give away treasured belongings and behave secretively,' Dr Daniel Fung told the conference. Not telling anyone was often a problem. Fung stressed the need to teach teenagers to recognise when their friends are in real trouble. He added, 'educating their peers is the most important because who knows teenagers best? It's their friends.'

How we cope and fail to cope

Britain pioneered child guidance and family therapy from the 1920s at clinics like the Tavistock in north London. In most of these clinics, the child's problems were not seen as isolated. It was not then a case of the evil out of control child against the good normal family. Many therapists insisted on seeing the whole family. This sensible and sensitive approach has been abandoned to a considerable extent.

To focus on just the sick child denies the complexity of family dynamics. Stress does not spark in a vacuum. Even if a child is depressed because he is being bullied at school, we need to ask why his parents seem so powerless to help him.

Parents need to provide safety and a stress-free zone. Mrs Thatcher once said that family was the one place where there was no bargaining. She was criticised for being naïve. It may be a rare example of the Iron Lady being idealistic. All too often, families are riddled with jealousy and competition.

Self Analysis 17
Seeing your child under stress is stressful – and often leads to unhelpful silences.
Are you frightened to raise serious issues with your kid?
Why?
Who can you discuss this with?

I discussed almost all of the issues below earlier but, as they are so important, I will repeat what seem to me key areas to probe once you steel yourself.

Self Analysis 18
Ask yourself:
Is your child being bullied at school?
Is she or he scared of failing at school?
Is there reason to worry you may be going to divorce?
Is your child worried about letting you down – and if so why?
Does one child feel you love another child more?
Does he or she hate their brother/sister/stepbrother for some reason?
Is she worried because she may be pregnant?
Has your child started to take drugs?

How can you help your child?

What can you do if you can see your child is under stress? The most basic rule is to talk, to make your child feel loved and to make her or him feel you can be trusted so they can confide in you. It often requires real determination and love to persevere but you will find the effort well worthwhile.

But if the problem is serious get help and, in the first instance, counselling or psychological help. Children do sometimes need medication but drugs by themselves will not cure deep-seated hurts or anxieties. Talking with an open heart and an open mind remains desperately important.

The games that they played making dolls at Prestwich brings me back to the start of this chapter. Sometimes imagination can help. Faced with the screaming child the Stanford Clinic called in a psychiatrist, David Spiegel. He came neither to medicate the patient nor to analyse but to play a game. He took her aside and asked her to trick the physicians by first imagining that a balloon tied to her wrist was taking her any place she wanted to go and then picturing having fun with her friends there. The eight-year-old got the idea. She returned to the consulting room and patiently endured the arduous check-up.

Spiegel and his colleagues have reported similar success with 21 children who need catheters. Diabetic and asthmatic kids also find this imaginative therapy useful according to Cindy Dell Clark of Pennsylvania State University. She interviewed 46 children, ages five to eight, who had either diabetes or asthma, and their parents; 45 of the children invented helpful rituals, playing with pretend friends. One diabetic boy endured his daily insulin injections by singing out 'Hallelujah!' – to the tune of the 'Hallelujah Chorus' in Handel's *Messiah* – as the needle pierced his skin. An asthmatic boy calmed himself if he had an attack by imagining that one of the Teenage Mutant Ninja Turtles had flown away to fetch the doctor.

20

Savvy kids don't come cheap

In 1983, advertisers spent $100 million on television advertising to kids. Today, they pour roughly 150 times that amount into TV, the internet and other media to persuade kids to spend what is not their money. Pressure, pressure, pressure for bling, bling and glam!

In China, the child market is reported to be worth $12 billion, in America over $40 billion. Apparently 80 per cent of all global brands now have a 'tween strategy'. In marketing jargon, *tweens* are children who are no longer tiny, but not yet teens. You go into your tweens around seven. Marketing mavens offer workshops on 'what works with kids and why', 'peer group marketing' and how to 'think like a kid'. Piaget, thou must be foaming in thy grave. What does the twenty-first-century human baby work towards? Being a mini Einstein? No. Being a major consumer. That, he or she must learn, is why we are on earth. To be a consumer. To spend, spend, spend. The credit crunch in 2009 is, many hope, a blip in our progress to consumer heaven.

Using mum and dad's money

The Swedes were the first to protest at the commercialisation of childhood. In 1994, the sociologist Erling Bjurström reported on the effects of TV commercials. Some children could understand the differences between programmes and ads but, he added: 'It is only by the age of 8 to 10 that most children have developed a basic understanding of the purpose of advertising. Furthermore research results indicate

Source: www.CartoonStock.com

that it is only around or after the age of 12 that we can be more certain that most children have developed a more complete understanding.' This work persuaded Sweden to ban TV ads aimed at children.

The rest of the world did not take much notice. The average American child is exposed to an estimated 40,000 television commercials a year – over 100 a day. A survey recently found that 27 per cent of American ads aimed at children and young people were for junk food. The next highest category – 10 per cent – was for military recruitment. Go to Iraq, eat Chunky-Choc and fight for Uncle Sam seems to be the message.

The not usually left wing American Psychological Association has gone Swedish and wants restrictions on advertising aimed at children under the age of eight. Younger children accept advertiser messages as truthful, accurate and unbiased it argues. The poor kids think they are some kind of public service announcement.

It is a controversial area because some psychologists argue that the anti-ad brigade are suffering a touch of the Piaget's and under-estimating kids. The media-literate child can spot the crucial messages that make an ad an ad, according to Brian Young, professor of psychology at Exeter University. He showed 66 children aged four to eight years two sorts of ads – the genuine article and doctored ads. The doctored ones had unusual punch-lines. One ad showed a face cream. The genuine version extolled the cream signing off that it made you better looking; the doctored version praised the cream but the punch-line was that it gave you disgusting spots.

Children aged four to five years liked the funny endings better and didn't notice whether or not the punch-lines made commercial sense. Six-year-olds reacted differently. Just over half understood there was something wrong with the funny endings but often couldn't say what it was.

All the eight-year-olds, however, had got the advertising game. They laughed at the doctored ads – not just because they were funny but because they were pathetic as ads. A face cream that gives you spots is not a product you'll sell, they pointed out.

The rise of new media – can my Blackberry connect with your iPod – makes children even more vulnerable. Kaiser Family Foundation research shows youth are multi-tasking their way through a variety of electronic media daily, juggling iPods and instant messaging with TV and cell phones. These never off some media kids pack 8.5 hours of media exposure into 6.5 hours each day, seven days a week.

The more they surf the net and the pod casts, the more kids absorb HAG, the Holy American Grail. Get your folks to buy our stuff. If they don't, they don't love you. The modern teen's theme song should be:

I just can't get enough
Of stuff, stuff, stuff!

By the time they are 3 years old, American children recognise over 100 brand logos. The attentive reader will not have forgotten the Dutch pundits who said dad is a piggybank. Dads who can't shell out often feel ashamed. A survey commissioned by the Centre for a New American Dream found children aged 12 to 17 ask their parents for products they have seen advertised an average of nine times until the parents finally give in. Over 10 per cent of 12- to 13-year-olds asked their parents more than 50 times for products they saw advertised. The correct way to deal with such consumer terrorism is to go with your child to the nearest shopping mall and threaten to take all your clothes off if they don't stop.

Sadly few dads have the moral courage – or figure – to do this. But it would be one hell of a protest. Don't be fooled by the notion the kids don't know stuff. They know enough to deny they're greedy pigs. They've learned the psychobabble. It's retail therapy, dad. And if I don't have the latest Star Battle Trike, none of my friends will talk to me.

More than half of the children under 12 surveyed (53 per cent) said that buying certain products made them feel better about themselves. And 12- to 13-year-olds are even sadder: 62 per cent say that buying certain products boosts their sense of self esteem. No one knows yet if the sub prime credit crunch has affected such attitudes.

But parents can spiel back. I love you to bits even if you don't have Boggle 3 or Auto Theft 9, now let's play chess. Or walk in the park. Or talk about cabbages and celebs.

At the centre of the media debate is the question of at what age do kids understand that an ad is not a normal programme but a message with just one purpose – to get you to buy stuff.

Professor Karen Pine of the University of Hertfordshire agrees with the Swedes who claimed that until they were six years old, children did not have any sense of the purpose of ads. Pine had the nice idea of looking at what toys children ask for in their letters to Santa. She and her colleagues also monitored toy advertising on TV in the six weeks before Christmas. Their results weren't surprising; the more TV children watch, the more toys they ask for in their letters to Santa. Children of four or five don't usually mention 'brand' names. They ask for a 'baby doll' but not 'Baby Annabel' by name.

By the time kids are six to eight years old, they are brand aware, brand literate, brand mad. They could work for an ad agency. They don't just ask for the advertised toys by brand name, they can even tell Santa which stores or sites he can buy them from and the retail price. Pine found a strong link between the amount of commercial TV six- to eight-year-olds watched, and the number of requests they made to Santa.

Pine claims, however, children who tell Santa where to go to buy the latest Smasho Basho still have not grasped that advertisers want one thing only – *your money*. Pine out-Swedes the Swedes and argues children are not consumer literate until they are even older, about 10 to 12. They get puberty before they get publicity. She adds: 'These kids, when we ask them, actually think ads are a kind of "public information" service. They think ads are shown to provide a comfort break between programs, or simply to tell us about what's in the shops.' Only *one* child aged four to eight out of a sample of 180 mentioned the fact that advertisers wanted to sell you stuff.

Girls asked Santa for more than boys. The reason, Pine suggests, may be that 'they are more verbal than boys at this age. Or because they are better senders and receivers of emotional messages, so are more able to process the persuasive content of adverts. Or maybe girls are socialized from an early age to shop and to believe that "you are what you own".'

Pine's analysis also showed ads suggest to children that they will be more popular if they own what's being spieled. Buy El Magnifica Doll and the ads show you playing with a happy group of friends. Ads do often show a child slightly older than their target market playing with the toy. Kids look up to older kids.

Spot the commercial

Given her views Pine suggests a game for parents to play with their children: 'Spot the Commercial'. While watching *Postman Pat* together, parents should tell their children the commercial truths that 'the people in the ads want Mom and Dad's money, that's what ads are for' (but that Mom and Dad will decide where it's best to spend their money). Then parents should confess they've been fooled by the evil ad-ders. Pine suggests parents should point out what happened when they fell for the spiel for Veel. 'It sure didn't get my floor *that* clean.'

Pine adds: 'We don't want to tell kids that TV lies, (but) simply make them less accepting of inflated claims.' She suggests parents hold out when the kids pester. And then there is the matter of resistance. 'As long as you always hold firm, they'll learn that pestering doesn't get them anywhere.' Good luck to you.

Finally Pine thinks technology can help harassed parents, arguing it is a good idea to tape kids' programmes ahead of time and show them how to fast-forward without ads (or use the facility to record without ads, if you have it). Involve children in buying decisions she also suggests.

Set a clear budget when shopping for items and teach them to look for good value for money. Encourage your children in all their non-TV related activities by getting out or engaging in hobbies, cooking, crafts and other activities with them.

I question some of Pine's findings, however. In 2000 I wrote a story for the *New Scientist* in which I interviewed researchers on kids marketing all over the world. Glen Smith of the Children's Research Unit in London did not accept children were as vulnerable as the Swedes suggested.

Smith claimed children who are much younger understand advertising. In one study, he showed commercials to four-year-olds. 'We had dolls representing children, mum, dad and so on. We asked the children to move the doll the ad was talking to forward. We found if there was a frozen pea commercial they moved the mum forward, if it was a toy they moved the child doll forward.' They got the message and who the sales pitch was aimed at.

Pine also seems to under-estimate the creativity of children. In 2000 and 2001, I was involved with two projects – the Victoria and Albert's brand-new exhibition and a BBC TV series *Shopology*. Both experiences suggested middle-class kids at least are brand and media literate. I filmed focus groups run by advertising agencies. What the children said made it clear that even seven-year-olds are often remarkably savvy about clothes, spending and fashion.

A smart ten-year-old, Harry said in one of these focus groups that his favourite brand was Reebok. When I said to him that a child's room is the same all over the world (which is a line Coca-Cola have used) and suggested they were trying to push the brand as a panacea, if you down a Coke, all your emotional needs will be met, Harry laughed.

'Rubbish,' Harry said, making it quite clear he understood the question just like an adult would.

'But why do you like Reebok?' I persisted.

He giggled. He didn't know why and he didn't care. His father put it down to peer pressure at school. Other parents suggested fear of bullying; children who have the right brands have status and so are less likely to be bullied.

Don't think you can fool us

Like Piaget, Pine seems to have under-estimated children. Merris Griffiths of Aberystwyth University showed TV ads to primary-school children in Wales. When they view ads for dolls and other toys, seven-year-old girls 'respond with surprising hostility. You'd think none of them had ever played with a Barbie doll,' Griffiths told me. But the older children are dismissive. 'I started showing groups of 7–11-year-olds ten selected ads for toys,' Griffiths told me. In all, she used ten ads – three for girls' toys, three for boys' and four neutral ones.

The children rejected the ads. Griffiths added: 'They felt insulted by them. The girls had the most hostile reactions. They were totally cynical.' This was as true of the seven-year-old girls as of the 11-year-old girls. 'They'd say things like "this is trickery",' she pointed out. The extent of the cynicism surprised her.

Griffiths argues advertisers use special techniques on television to counter the knowingness of children. A content analysis of 20 TV ads showed the ads are 'gendered'; subtle techniques are used to appeal in different ways to boys or girls. Ads for boys' toys use far more high angle shots. She saw this as emphasising their superiority. Ads for girls' toys use far more low angle shots. Ads for boys' toys are paced faster and use cuts far more than dissolves.

These techniques – especially the prevalence of cuts over dissolves – may not sound sinister. Professor John Murray of Kansas State University thinks otherwise. Murray was part of a 1992 American Psychological Association working party on children and television. On mainstream television, Murray told me: 'the time for children's programmes is quite limited so ads have to appeal to a wide age group. The problem with children's programmes is that most are aimed at a very broad age group – around 2 to 12. There's only one way you can keep the attention of both 2- and 12-year-olds and that is to have very fast-paced fast-action programmes.'

Murray has analysed American programmes on Saturday mornings, a key period for children. Most are cartoons with fast cuts and fast action. The easiest way of achieving fast pace is violence, Murray said. The average number of violent events in an hour of children's television includes 24 deaths as opposed to five deaths per hour on prime-time TV. 'Laughter goes along with many of these deaths – and I just can't think that's good.' In 2000, Murray predicted pressure in the wake of the Columbine school shootings to curb violence in programmes and ads but that has not happened.

Pine claims advertisers use cartoons not for good reasons. 'Even though research has shown cartoons can diminish a child's attention span in the longer term, advertisers will always put their sales figures before your child's welfare,' Pine denounces.

Yet children can be so aware of what sells that advertising agencies use focus groups to get ideas for new products.

How do kids know about royalties?

The children in one focus group were asked to design a new cereal. A group of 10–12-year-olds came up with the name Eat My Shorts based on Bart Simpson's well-known quip. The packaging would be in the shape of shorts. The kids even discussed the royalties they would have to pay to the creators of The Simpsons. They also liked the idea of inserting various add-ons so you would sprinkle chocolate flakes, for example, on cereal.

This research suggests one troubling trend, troubling for advertisers, at least. Almost as soon as children understand what advertising is about, they become hostile to it. Paradoxically, this hostility doesn't seem to stop them enjoying the ads. Nor, sadly, does it stop them spending money stupidly.

Griffiths' findings also made her worry about violence. The Welsh children enjoyed car ads much more than toy ads. 'They seemed to treat them more as light entertainment than as advertising.' Griffiths was struck by how most of her subjects responded to an ad for the Citroen Saxo. This ad has animation where the strong Saxo survives being rammed, booted and attacked. The violence is funny. But what impressed Griffiths was 'how much the children loved it'.

Belch, Flurry and teen mavens

A final point. According to Belch and Willis Flurry (Belch *et al.*, 2005) – yes, those are their real names and they work at San Diego State University – the internet is giving kids more power when families make decisions, including decisions about shopping. We all shop online now. Many kids find that easy – their fingers live on the keyboard – while many keyboard challenged grown ups don't know how to navigate sites any more than they know how to navigate at sea. Little Joe may not know Paris is the capital of France, but he does know how to get on *ebay*, *Amazon* or *Shop till Dad is Broke*.

Belch *et al.* refer to these know-all kids as teen internet 'mavens', a Yiddish term for expert. The mavens enjoy net surfing and have more influence in the family decision-making process than non-maven teens.

So just as soon as your toddler stops pestering you to buy, your teen starts bargaining with you. If you want me to find you the best deal for that weekend break you and mum want to take, you'll have to buy me a new CD or the latest add-on to the latest game.

21

Who is the child?

I have explained how home left me but most of my generation could not leave home fast enough. The last thing we wanted to do was live with our parents. Most of my friends left home when they were 18. After university, they did not come home. Psychologists used to worry about how the 'empty nesters' felt after their children had left home.

It has all changed and the nest or flat or semi-detached is not empty at all. There are a number of reasons. Some children never leave home; some hare back after uni; some have to come back because their marriage/civil partnership/ relationship has broken down. More children live at home as 20 somethings, 30 somethings and even 40 somethings probably than since the Middle Ages or, to be more sensible, since the 1960s.

It is the natural course for the young to leave the nest, mate and then create new nests of their own. Now that this is not happening we are seeing what I call *the dependency paradox*. It works two ways. First, young people remain too dependent on their parents for too long; secondly, we are seeing parents becoming dependent on their children.

Vicky Houston of the University of Sunderland reported a longitudinal study for the Economic and Social Science Research Council. She analysed data on 17,000 people born in a single week – some in 1958, some in 1970. Of the sample born in 1970 – who were in their early thirties – one in six men have never left the family home, or returned there. That is double the number of those born in 1958 (Houston, 2004). And the statistics for those born after 1990 will be even higher. It sometimes seems that young people today only mature by the time they are 35 because we all grow up more slowly.

The 'good enough', 'mug enough' parent provides decent food, decent drink, television, fully integrated music centres, personal computers, the phone and, of course, the roof over the head. Add a shoulder to cry on and no rent to pay. One result is tension – and the other is infantilisation. You can't be truly grown up, you can't be truly independent, while you are still living in your parents' house.

At the same time, some parents seem to be making inappropriate emotional demands of their children. In 2005, Synovate, an American market research firm, surveyed 1,000 parents who had children aged 12 to 30 living at home; 43 per cent of the parents said they wanted to be their child's best friend. The problem with that seemingly lovely ambition is that a mum or a dad needs to be more than, and different from, a friend. Friends should be equals; parents should not try to be or pretend they are just a mate. According to Synovate's Chief Executive, Sam Pierpoint, the best-friend parent 'doesn't give you rules and tell you what to do'.

Intrigued, Pierpoint spent time with 45 families and was shocked to find standards had fallen. Some parents didn't insist their teens did homework; one mother said doing homework would make her son unhappy. Other parents didn't make the kids do any chores. They didn't want to upset the fragile little 20-year-old darlings. Some 20 somethings interviewed by Synovate had never paid their own bills or bought personal items like deodorant or toothpaste. One young man didn't know how to make coffee. 'We call them "adult-escents". They are 25 years old but have the life skills of a teenager,' Pierpoint said.

Many parents felt their own parents didn't understand them and wanted to be closer to their children. The Synovate survey concluded that many parents today view their kids as 'emotional assets, the objects of their love and affection' and rely too much on them. Many parents also want '"quality time" with their children to be friendly and non-confrontational.' Some parents share personal and work-related problems with their children because they don't live near their own parents or friends. If parents depend on their children for comfort, I would argue, it is one of those bad nexuses which will end up making many therapists rich.

Then, there are life's little hassles. In the old days, if you had to go back home, you lived on Ma and Pa's terms. You certainly couldn't bring boys or girls home to stay the night without complex negotiations. Even after Aileen and I were engaged, when we stayed with her parents we were put in separate bedrooms. I had been able to have girls to stay after my mother came back from Israel only because she had totally lost the moral high ground having flitted off to foreign parts and her lover for three years.

But, today, the parent who wants to stop a son or daughter having someone back to stay the night has to be willing to have a fight.

Separate bedrooms? What are you, dad? The Pope?

It is telling that the dependent young have no intention of being caught out in the same way by their own kids. In the Synovate survey, a 22-year-old man said: 'There's no way I'm going to be like my mom. My mom does everything for me. She's made me lazy. There is no way the kids are going to rule my house. I'm going to be a bad-ass parent.'

Self Analysis 19
What was the most adult thing your parents asked you to do?
How did you respond?
Did you feel it was too much of an imposition because you were still a child?

Little Harriett's just like me

I suspect there are at least two reasons why some parents do not insist on 'their rights' when a child in his twenties, or even thirties, lives at home. One is that we, too, are confused; the second is that the dependency paradox is tempting. Letting go of your children is not easy. If they want to stay at home, you feel flattered. It proves you are a good parent, their best friend, so the temptation is to cling on to them and let them behave badly while clinging on to you.

In the first chapter, I looked at the age-old ambivalence between fathers and sons dating back to Abraham and Isaac. Psychoanalysts suggest sometimes the conflicts are due to narcissism – the father sees himself in his son and the son will carry on 'my' essence. If my son is not only biologically like me but psychologically like me, I will be truly powerful and immortal.

In the preface to *Common Sense and the Child*, the radical educator A.S. Neill (1967) wrote of the fate of children with strong fathers. He said:

> And because Daddy is possessive and likes radio and polished pianos, he takes it for granted that little Jimmy, being made in his father's image, has the same interests . . . This leads to the most disastrous warping of the child's boy nature for the boy is nearly always sacrificed to the grand piano.

My father was deeply disappointed when I did not follow in his footsteps and become a lawyer like him. I had decided to leave school at 16 to become an actor. But my father was supportive and smart. For months, he came down to Mine-head every week to see me play in seaside rep. I was the police sergeant in *Getaway with Murder*, a daft whodunit, the ten-year-old wisecracking New York kid in *Critic's Choice* and a village idiot in an unspeakable play about sheep stealing in Wales. The man who had left me home alone now changed into a good dad; he was not a bad critic. He had the sense to let me try to be an actor though he saw that I'd never be a second Laurence Olivier.

If my father had not been wise, I suspect I would have struggled on for years trying to be an actor. If only to prove my father wrong. As it was, after two years of failing auditions and the occasional crummy part, I gave up acting. My father couldn't contain his joy. I went to Oxford. He might have screwed up but I always loved and respected him for his good sense about giving up what was an ambition for him, I suspect. That I should be a lawyer as he had been before his career went wrong.

I became a psychologist, writer and director and, ironically, I never acted again till 2002. And here comes the ambivalent bit. Who was it who cast me in my first part for 30 years in *Beginner's Luck*? My son Nicholas. Well, you will have spotted the flaw. For my son to cast me he had to be a director. I believe I neither pushed him nor discouraged him but I'm probably fooling myself. Thanks to Nicholas, I was back playing a policeman as in *Getaway with Murder* when I was 16.

I was, of course, pathetically flattered my son wanted me to be in his film. It is all too human to want your children to be like you, all too human and all too stupid. My other son Reuben is a writer and editor but I can't be blamed entirely for that. His mother is also a writer.

I did not expect this book to be so personal. I have found writing about the father–child relationship made me think, and made me remember, much about my father, my mother and about my children. Maybe it was naïve of me to think it wouldn't. Being a father is not a subject one can be simply objective about. I hope readers will have found the text amusing, moving and helpful. I do not claim to have been a good father but I have tried to be a good enough father. I have certainly learned that the hopes, fears, joys, irritations, angers, moments of love, love given, love got, that happen between a father and his children are the very stuff of life. I thank my children for that.

If you are not yet a father, prepare for it, look forward to it, it is one of the joys of life. If you are a dad, struggling with the nappies/homework/bills/life, pause if you are feeling stressed. My mother-in-law was right. The kids may be a pain in the neck, but they are the only real immortality we get.

Organisations and resources

Organisations

Organisations for fathers have tended to be militant, fighting for the rights of fathers involved in custody battles.

Fathers who need advice in less aggressive situations may find the following organisations more useful.

Enquire (Scotland). Enquire is the Scottish advice service for additional support for learning, providing independent advice and information to parents/carers, children/young people and the adults who support them. It is managed by Children in Scotland and funded by the Scottish Executive. Email: info@enquire.org.uk

Families Need Fathers, 134 Curtain Road, London EC2A 3AR – more in the line of fighting for the rights of fathers.

HomeDad.org.uk – who provide advice for fathers who are at home.

National Childbirth Trust. The NCT is one of the UK's leading charities for parents. It has a good website: www/nctpregnancyandbabycare.com. It also has a phone line: 0300 33 00 770.

Parentline Plus – phone 0800800222 for general advice.

The traditional charities like NSPCC and the Children's Society, though they do not specifically deal with advice for fathers, provide excellent general literature on what children need.

Some useful books/videos

Helping Children Learn. Leaflets giving ideas on how to support children through different stages of their school years includes pre-school; school age; helping with home-work; families and schools; and changing schools. Single leaflets free, multiple copies 20p each. Contact Parentline Plus, centraloffice@parentlineplus.org.uk, website: www. parentlineplus.org.uk.

Helping Children with . . . A series of five guides presenting information in an accessible way in order to support parents. Topics covered are reading, spelling, maths, reading difficulties and handwriting. They are pro-duced by the National Centre for Language and Literacy, University of Reading, Bulmershe Court, Reading RG6 1HY. Website: www.ncll.org.uk.

Videos. The text mentions a number of films made by the author – especially on the work on Stephen Ceci and *The Last Taboo*, a study of child abuse. Further information from dcpsychologynews@gmail.com

Thanks to Rebekah Edmondson for useful comments and critiques, to Dawn Harris for skill and patience in seeing it through to print – I do some publishing so I know how awful authors can be – and thanks to four dads who offered interesting views and critiques – Martin Hay, David Carr Brown. Kessup Choe, Alex Lynford.

References

Astrachan, A., (1978). *How Men Feel*. New York: Anchor Books.

Baron Cohen, S., (2008). *Autism and Asperger's Syndrome*. Oxford: Oxford University Press.

Bartrip, J., Morton, J., De Schonen, S., (2001). Responses to mother's face in 3-week to 5-month-old infants. *British Journal of Developmental Psychology*, 19 (2), pp.219–232.

Bartsch, K. and Wellman, H., (1995). *Children Talk About the Mind*. Oxford: Oxford University Press.

Baumrind, D., (1988). *Rearing Competent Children*. San Francisco: Jossey Bass.

Belch, M., Krentler, K.A. and Willis-Flurry, L., (2005). Teen internet mavens: influence in family decision making. *Journal of Business Research*, 58, 569–575.

Belsky, J. and Pensky, E., (1988). *Transitions to Parenthood*. Philadelphia: Haworth Press.

Benton, D. and Roberts, G., (1988). Effects of vitamin supplementation on intelligence of a sample of schoolchildren. *Lancet*, 1, 140–44.

Blendis, J., (1988). *Paternal involvement in childcare*. Ph D Dissertation, University of London.

Bower, T., (1989). *The Rational Infant*. New York: WH Freeman.

Bowlby, J., (1981). *Attachment and Loss*. Harmondsworth: Penguin.

Brazelton, T., (1994). *Touchpoints: The Essential Reference*. Boston, MA: Addison-Wesley.

Carr, D., (2008). *The Night of the Gun*. New York: Simon and Schuster.

Centers for Disease Control and Prevention (2005). *Morbidity and Mortality Weekly Report*, 1 August.

Chan, K.K.L. and Paterson-Brown, S., (2002). How do fathers feel after accompanying their partners in labour and delivery? *Journal of Obstetrics and Gynaecology*, 22(1), 11–15.

Chess, S. and Thomas, A., (1986). *Temperament in Clinical Practice*. New York: Guilford Press.

Chomsky, N., (1957). *Syntactic Structures*. The Hague: Mouton.

Chomsky, N., (1986). *Knowledge of Language: Its Nature, Origin and Use*. Westport, CT: Praeger

Cohen, D., (1977). *Psychologists on Psychology*. London: Routledge.

Cohen, D., (1994. *The Development of Play*. London: Routledge.

Cohen, D., (2005). *Psychologists on Psychology* (3rd revised ed.). London: Edward Arnold.

Coleman, J.C., (1974). *Relationships in Adolescence*. London: Routledge.

Cook, J. and Bewley, S.J., (2008). Acknowledging a persistent truth: domestic violence in pregnancy. *Royal Society of Medicine*, 101, 358–363.

Corby, B., (ed) (2000). *Child Abuse*. Milton Keynes: Open University Press.

Crowell, S.E., Beauchaine, T.P., McCauley, E., Smith, C.J., Stevens, A.L. and Sylvers, P., (2004). Psychological, autonomic and serotonergic correlates of parasuicide among adolescent girls. *Development and Psychopathology*, 17, 1105–1127.

Curry, N.E. and Arnaud, S., (1974). Play in preschool settings . In T. Yawkey and A. Pellegrini (eds) *Child's Play*. New Jersey: Lawrence Erlbaum Associates, Inc.

De Courcy, A., (2008). *Snowdon: The Biography*. London: Weidenfeld and Nicholson.

Delahunty, K.M., McKay, D.W., Noseworthy, D.E. and Storey, A.E., (2007, online December 5, 2006). Prolactin responses to infant cues in men and women: effects of parental experience and recent infant contact. *Hormones and Behavior*, 51(2), 213–220.

Elliott, L., (1995). *Compulsive Murders*. Toronto: McClelland and Stewart.

Fagan, J., Iglesias, A., (1999). Father involvement program effects on fathers, father figures and their Head Start children: A quasi-experimental study. *Early Childhood Research Quarterly*, 14, 243–269.

Fantz, R.L., (1970). Visual perception and experience in infancy: Issues and approaches. In: D. Lindsley and F. Young (eds.) *Early Experience and Visual Information Processing in Perceptual and Reading Disorders*. *National Academy of Sciences*; 351–380.

Feiring, D., (1976). The Influence of the Child and Secondary Characteristics. *American Academy of Child Psychiatry*, 15, 414–429.

Freud, S., (1913). *Totem and Taboo*. London: The Hogarth Press.

Freud, S., (1940). *An Outline of Psychoanalysis*. London: The Hogarth Press.

Gaskins, S., Haight, W. and Lancy, D.F., (2007). The cultural construction of play. In A. Göncü and S. Gaskins (eds.) *Play and Development: Evolutionary, Sociocultural and Functional Perspectives*. New Jersey: Lawrence Erlbaum Associates, Inc.

Gibbins, J. and Thomson, A.M., (2001). Women's expectations and experiences of childbirth. *Midwifery*, 17(4), 302–313.

Gopnik, A., Meltzoff, A. and Kuhl, P., (2001. *How Babies Think: The Science of childhood*. London: Phoenix Press.

Gorell Barnes, G., Thompson, P., Daniel, G and Burkhardt, N., (1998). *Growing up in Stepfamilies*. Oxford: Clarendon Press.

Graziano, A.M. and Namaste, K.A., (1990). Parental use of physical force in child discipline. *Journal of Interpersonal Violence*, 5(4), 449—463

Griffin, W., (1998). *Fathers without Fail*. ASU Research website: www.ovprea.asu.ed

Grimm-Wassil, C., (1994). *Where's Daddy?* New York: Overlook Press.

Gunter, B. and McAleer, S., (1990). *Children and Television: The One-Eyed Monster?* London: Routledge.

Guterman, N. and Lee, Y., (2005). The Role of Fathers in Risk for Physical Child Abuse and Neglect: Possible Pathways and Unanswered Questions. *Child Maltreatment*, 10, 136–149.

Haddon, M., (2004). *The Curious Incident of the Dog in the Night Time*. London: Vintage.

Harvey, A., (1980). The parent infant relationship. *Journal of the Royal Society of Medicine*, 73, 339–352.

Harris, P.L., (2000). *The Work of the Imagination*. Oxford: Blackwell.

Hayward, J. and Chalmers, B., (1990). Obstetricians' and mothers' perceptions of obstetric events. *Journal of Psychosomatic Obstetrics and Gynaecology*, 11(1), 57–71.

Healy, D., (2004). *The Creation of Psychopharmacology*. Cambridge, MA: Harvard University Press.

Henneborn, W.J. and Cogan, R., (1975). The effect of husband participation in reported pain and the probability of medication during labor and birth. *Journal of Psychosomatic Research*, 19, 215–222.

Hepper, P., (1991). An examination of fetal learning before and after birth. *Irish Journal of Psychology*, 12 (2), 95–107.

Herbert, M., (1987). *Living with Teenagers*. Oxford: Blackwell.

Hine, T., (1999). *The Rise and Fall of the American Teenager*. New York: Avon.

Houston, V., (2004). Report on an ESRC longditudinal study (*The Sunday Herald*, June 20, 2004, Jenifer Johnston).

Huggins, M., (2009). *I'll Love You If:*. London: Psychology News Press.

Ip, W.Y., (2000). Relationship between partner's support during labour and maternal outcomes. *Journal of Clinical Nursing*, 9, 265–272.

Johnson, M.P., (2002). The implications of unfulfilled expectations and perceived pressure to attend the birth on men's stress levels following birth attendance: a longitudinal study. *Journal of Psychosomatic Obstetrics and Gynaecology*, 23(3),173–182.

Joseph, R.M. and Tager Flusberg, H., (1999). Preschool children's understanding of desire and the constraints of an intended action. *British Journal of Developmental Psychology*, 17, 221–243

Kagan, J., (1994). *Galen's Prophecy Temperament in Human Nature*. Jackson, TN: Westview Press.

Kavanaugh, R.D. and Harris, P.L., (2003). Pretence and counterfactual thoughts in young children. In L. Balter and C. Tamis-Lemonda (eds) *Child Psychology: A Handbook of Contemporary Issues*. London: Psychology Press.

Kiernan, K., (2006). Non-residential fatherhood and child involvement: evidence from the Millenium Cohort Study. *Journal of Social Policy*, 35(4), 1–19.

Kiernan, K. and Smith, K., (2003). Unmarried parenthood: new insights from the Millennium Cohort Study. *Population Trends*, 114, 26–33. London: Office of Population, Censuses and Surveys.

Klein, R.P., Gist, N.E., Nicholson, J. and Standley, K., (1981). A study of father and nurse support during labour. *Birth and the Family Journal*, 8, 161–164.

Kohlberg, L., (1984). *The Psychology of Moral Development*. New York: Harper and Row.

Kojima, K., Nomiyama, M., Kumamoto, T., Matsumoto., Y. and Iwasaka, T., (2001). Transvaginal ultrasound-guided embryo transfer, improves pregnancy and implantation rates after IVF. *Human Reproduction*, 16(12), 2578–2582.

Kraebel, K., (2009). *The Infant Learning and Memory Project*. http://web.cortland.edu/kraebelk or contact Kimberly Kraebel at (607) 753–2045.

Lamb, M. and Tamis-Lemonda, C., (2004). *Fathers Matter*. Chichester: John Wiley.

Lemos, G., (2004). *Fear and Fashion: The Use of Knives and Other Weapons by Young People*. London: Lemos and Crane.

Lessing, E. Zagorin, S.W and Nelson, D.D., (1970). WISC subtest and IQ score correlates of father absence. *Journal of Genetic Psychology*, 67, 181–195.

Lewis, C. and O'Brien, M., (1987). *Reassessing Fatherhood: New*

Observations on Fathers and the Modern Family. London: Sage Publications Ltd.

McBride, B.A., Bae, J. and Rane, T.R., (2001). Family-school partnerships in prekindergarten at-risk programs: An exploratory study. In S. Redding and L. Thomas (eds.), *The Community of the School* (pp. 229–245). Lincoln, IL: The Academic Institute.

Mackintosh, N.J., (1999). *IQ and Human Intelligence* Oxford: Oxford University Press.

Masson, J., (1999). *The Emperor's Embrace*. London: Penguin.

Max Planck Institute (2005). *Munich Encounters in Cognition and Action*. Munchen: Max Planck Institute.

Meltzoff, A.N. and Moore, M.K., (1983). Newborn infants imitate adult facial gestures. *Child Development*, 54, 702–709.

Miles, R., (1994). *The Children We Deserve*. London: Harper Collins.

Miyake, K., Chen, S. and Campos, J., (1985). Infant temperament and mother's mode of interaction and attachment in Japan; an interim report. In I. Bretherton and E Waters (eds), Growing points of attachment theory and research. *Monographs of the Society for Research in Child Development*, 50, 276–297.

Morris, D., (2008). *The Naked Man*. London: Vintage.

Moore, T. and Kotelchuck, M., (2004). Predictors of urban fathers' involvement in their child's health care. *Pediatrics*, 113(3), 574–580.

Moser, C., (1998). *A fresh start. The report of the working group chaired by Sir Claus Moser*. UK: Department for Educations and Skills.

Neill, A.S., (1967). *Talking of Summerhill*. London: Gollancz.

Nelson, C., (2007). *Family Ties in Victorian England: Victorian Life and Times*. Connecticut: Praeger Publishing Inc.

NFO System Three for Scottish Executive (2002). *Disciplining Children: Research with Parents in Scotland*.

National Health Service (2005). *NHS Maternity Services Quantitative Research* (October), prepared by TNS System Three for Kate Hawkins, Department of Health, London.

Odent, M., (1999). Is the father's participation at birth dangerous? *Midwifery Today*, 51, 23–24..

Palermo, G. and Ross, L.G., (1999). Mass murder, suicide and moral development. *International Journal of Offender Therapy*, 43, 8–20.

Parke, R.D., (2002). Fathers and Families. In M.H. Bornstein *Handbook of Parenting*. New Jersey: Lawrence Erlbaum Associates, Inc.

Piaget, J., (1950). *The Psychology of Intelligence*. London: Routledge.

Piaget, J., (1952). *Play, Dreams and Imitation in Childhood*. London: Routledge.

Reissland, N., (1988). Neonatal imitation in the first hour of life: observations in rural Nepal. *Developmental Psychology*, 24, 464–469.

Reyna, V.F. and Farley, F., (2006). Risk and Rationality in Adolescent Decision Making: Implications for Theory, Practice and Public Policy. *Psychological Science in the Public Interest*, 7(1), 1–44.

Reyna, V.F. and Farley, F., (2006/2007). Is the teen brain too rational? *Scientific American Mind*, December/January.

Saisto, T., Salmela-Aro, K., Nurmi, J.E. and Halmesmaki, E., (2001). CS: Caesarean section. *Acta Obstetricia et Gynecologica Scandinavica*, 80.

Salthouse, T., (1998). Pressing Issues in Cognitive Ageing. In N Schwarz (ed) *Cognition Ageing and Self*. New Jersey: Lawrence Erlbaum Associates, Inc.

Schmidt, L. and Fox, N., (1998). Fear potentiated startle response in temperamentally different infants. *Developmental Psychobiology*, 32, 113–121.

Sharon, T. and Woolley, J.D., (2004). Do monsters dream? Young children's understanding of the fantasy/reality distinction. *British Journal of Developmental Psychology*, 22, 293–310

Sheehan, M. and Watson, M., (2008). Reciprocal influences between maternal discipline techniques and aggression in children and adolescents. *Aggressive Behavior*, 34(3), 245—255.

Singh, D. and Newburn, M., (2000). *Becoming a Father*. London: National Childbirth Trust.

Smetana, J.G., Metzger, A. and Campione-Barr, N., (2004). African-American late adolescents' relationships with parents: developmental transitions and longitudinal patterns. *Child Development*, 75(3), 932—947.

Spelke, E.S., (2007). Innéisme, liberté et langage. In J. Bricmont and J. Franck (eds), *Cahier no 88: Noam Chomsky*. Paris: L'Herne (pp 818–187).

Storo, J. and Jansen, A., (2006). *The Norwegian man as father*. Paper at www.childresearch net

Straus, M.A. and Donnelly, M.K., (2004). *Beating the Devil Out of Them: Corporal Punishment in American Families and its Effects on Children*. Lexington, MA: Lexington Press.

Sully, J., (1912). *Studies of Childhood*. London: Longmans.

Tannen, D., (1991). *You Just Don't Talk*. London: Vintage.

Valentine, C.W., (1942). *The Normal Child*. Harmondsworth: Penguin.

Verschueren, K. and Marcoen, A., (1999). Representation of self and socioemotional competences in kindergarteners. *Child Development*, 70, 183–201.

Watson, J.B. and Watson, R., (1928). *Psychological Care of Infant and Child*. London: George Allen & Unwin.

Wei-Chung Allen Lee (2008). *Journal for the Public Library of Science (PLOS) Biology*, 27 December.

Williams, E. and Radin, N., (1999). Effects of father participation in child rearing: twenty year follow-up. *American Journal of Orthopsychiatry*, 69, 328 – 336.

Winnicott, D.W., (1953). Transitional objects and transitional phenomena. *International Journal of Psychoanalysis*, 34, 89–97.

Young Minds (2008). *Teens Cause Parents Greatest Concern*. www.youngminds.org.uk (released 6 August).

Yu, C. and Smith, L., (2008). Infants rapidly learn word referent mappings. *Cognition*, 106, 1558–1568.

Zahn Waxler, C., Radke-Yarrow, M. and King, R., (1979). Child rearing and children's prosocial intentions towards victims of distress. *Child Development*, 50, 319–330.

Index